A DOG IS A DOG
and That's Why He's So Special

CLARICE RUTHERFORD

A Dog Is A Dog
and That's Why He's So Special

CLARICE RUTHERFORD

Alpine
PUBLICATIONS
Crawford, CO

A DOG IS A DOG: And That's Why He's So Special

ISBN 10: 1-57779-103-7
ISBN 13: 978-1-57779-103-4
Cataloging in Publication

Rutherford, Clarice.
   A dog is a dog : and that's why he's so special / by Clarice Rutherford.
      p. cm.
   Includes bibliographical references
   ISBN-13: 978-2-57779-103-4 (pbk. : alk. paper)
   ISBN-10: 1-57779-103-7 (pbk. : alk. paper)
  1. Dogs--Behavior--Juvenile literature. 2. Dogs--Training--Juvenile
literature. I. Title
  SF 433.R88 2012
  636. 7'0887-dc22

The information contained in this book is complete and accurate to the best of our knowledge. All recommendations are made without guarantee on the part of the author or Alpine Publications, Inc. The author and publisher disclaim any liability with the use of this information.

For the sake of simplicity, the terms he or she are sometimes used to identify an animal or person. These are used in the generic sense only. No discrimination of any kind is intended toward either sex.

Cover Design: Gary Raham, Biostration
Cover Art: Hiroko Ishimura
Editing: Deb Helmers
Layout: Laura Newport
Photographs by Clarice Rutherford and Kelly Hines Keller.
Illustrations: NJ Wiley

1 2 3 4 5 6 7 8 9 0

Printed in the United States of America.

CONTENTS

CONTENTS

CONTENTS

The dog has changed over time. It is our responsibility to make sure that dogs continue to be "man's best friend."

When I named this book it wasn't because the title was short and simple. I had reasons. I want to tell you what I was thinking about.

"A Dog Is A Dog." What does this mean? It means he is an animal on planet Earth unlike any other. Long ago humans opened the door to the wild and the wolf invited itself in. Some of those wolves chose to stay close to humans. Over time these wolves became domesticated and developed into the dog. Researchers determined that the domestication of the dog from the wolf was in process about 12,000 years ago. Archaeologists first found dog bones along with human bones in ancient ruins dated back to that time.

Even though the dog is now a separate species from the wolf, to know the dog you must first know the wolf. Certain traits continue to be part of a dog's behavior. These instincts are often the reason why dogs act like they do. When you know of these instincts and what sets them off, you can teach your dog how to control his reaction to them. This, in turn, helps your dog respect you and look to you for guidance to understand his place in the family pack.

"And That's Why He's So Special." What does this mean? The dog chose to offer what he can to humans, beyond what they give to each other – a bonding where the dog always knows the feelings of his person – no need for words or woofs. When something happens and you feel like you're living in a shadow, your dog knows. When someone at school says "Thanks a lot" and smiles, or you kick in a soccer goal and you're on a cloud, your dog knows. This is what makes a dog so special. He's there for you if you allow him.

Your dog needs to know that you're there for him, too. To share this specialness you need to spend time with him. It won't always be as long as you would like, and he won't always behave as you would like, but together you learn from each other and that's what's so special for you both.

ACKNOWLEDGEMENTS

My thanks to Barbara Fleming for her amazing organizing abilities, to the Friday Writers' Group for their continued support, to my husband, Bill, and to all the dogs who have lived with us during the years and enriched our lives immeasurably.

chapter one

IT'S A DOG'S LIFE

Buster, a brown and white shepherd-type dog, always held his own in a fight. Nicky, reddish brown, wiry, with a sharp face, lived across the street from Buster. Nicky had lost his left front foot in a trap. They were best buddies.

Up the street lived Rocky, a big black dog. Buster and Nicky liked to tease him. Buster and Nicky went out into the street, put their heads together and stood like that. A big bush grew at the edge of the street near Buster's house. Buster hid behind the bush. Then Nicky went up the street to antagonize Rocky into chasing him.

Down the street they came as fast as Nicky could run on three legs. Rocky caught up to Nicky about the time they reached the bush. Buster leaped out from his hiding place and nailed Rocky as he went by. They rolled over and over in the dusty street, with Buster snarling and growling. The fight never lasted long. Rocky gave up quickly and ran home screeching, his tail between his legs. Buster and Nicky stood out in the street bumping heads, wagging their tails, obviously giving high fives. They could always count on Rocky.

Those carefree but risky dog days are long gone. Today, a dog's life is very different.

These scenes took place in a small Colorado town before it had leash laws. Buster, Nicky, Rocky and their dog friends were free to roam around the town, congregate and socialize—free to follow their nature.

Still, life wasn't all fun and games for Buster, Nicky and Rocky. Even though small-town life for dogs was very social, with many people and dog friends, it also had its disadvantages. Distemper was a common viral disease, often fatal. Dogs weren't often taken to a veterinarian for injuries or distemper vaccinations. If a puppy in a litter survived distemper, which was very contagious, it was often left with problems such as convulsions, weak lungs and sometimes lameness.

Dogs also got hurt in their travels about town. Nicky caught his foot in a coyote trap, and dogs that chased cars sometimes got hit. Curious puppies found all sorts of mischief that caused pain and grief, and of course there were always skunks and porcupines. Families did what they could to help their dogs get well but the dogs were always vulnerable.

Barking is a natural behavior of dogs which can irritate your neighbors. Dogs must be taught not to bark unnecessarily.

Those carefree but risky dog days are long gone. Today, a dog's life is very different. Laws and restrictions limit dogs' freedom.

Learning why dogs do what they do will help people teach their dogs what they need to know. People will learn what they must do: clean up after their dogs on walks and work on the barking problem. Instead of being restricted, perhaps even removed, dogs will be accepted and welcomed in our communities.

Living in the 21st century presents new challenges to dogs and their families, especially those living in cities. Barking dogs irritate neighbors. Neighbors don't like picking up dog messes left in their yards. Stepping in dog messes is extremely irritating. A misbehaving dog, for example one that runs loose or jumps on people or other dogs, can result in Animal Control coming to take that dog to the shelter.

If we don't want dogs to be very restricted or forbidden in our neighborhoods and towns, we must learn about the effects of their inherited wolf instincts. Learning why dogs do what they do will help people teach their dogs what they need to know. People will learn what they must do: clean up after their dogs on walks and work on the barking problem. Instead of being restricted, perhaps even removed, dogs will be accepted and welcomed in our communities.

Although they can't have the freedom dogs once did, we can help the dogs of today learn to live happily in the 21st century, even with all the limitations and human expectations there are now, and still be true to their heritage.

LOOSE DOGS

Our dogs should never be allowed to run loose in any city, suburb or farm area. Traffic is a constant threat, even to those who appear to be street-wise. Wandering dogs can also be a threat to people. Drivers can cause an accident when they swerve to miss a dog. People walking on sidewalks can also be injured by dogs not on a leash. They might be bumped or knocked down by an overly enthusiastic dog who is running toward another dog.

A serious situation happens when a loose dog sees something, and we don't know what, that triggers the prey instinct. Perhaps it is a small dog being held in her person's arms, or a cat. Corky, who is the best dog in the world at home, can jump for the little dog and cause fear and injuries to the person.

Dogs should always be walked on a leash.

If your dog gets out by accident, you should have a license tag on the collar and a tag that has your name and phone number on it. Someone could get in touch with you so that you can go and get your dog. The best solution is to never leave your yard gate unlatched or leave a door open. But those things do happen once in a while, so be prepared for what to do. As long as your dog has a tag, whoever finds Corky can call you. You can also phone your local animal shelter to see if Corky is there.

MYTHS

There are many myths to explain the relationship between humans and animals, especially dogs. This one comes from a Native American tribe:

Long, long ago humans lived in harmony with nature. By using telepathy, they communicated with other animals. One day the Great Spirit placed Human apart from the animals. The Great Spirit then began to open a huge chasm in the earth to make this separation permanent. Dog looked at Human and then turned back to his animal friends. The chasm grew wider. Dog again looked at Human, but again turned back to his animal friends. The chasm grew wider still. Finally, at the last possible moment before the chasm was too wide to jump, Dog took a mighty leap and forever joined with Human. It is that way to this day.

Through the many millennia of time that the dog has lived in the company of humans an unbreakable bond has developed.

chapter two

FROM A WOLF TO A DOG

Look into a wolf's eyes. See the wild: not crazy wild but the wild of being free, of having the instincts for survival during years of extreme drought and years of bitter cold. See the wolf legs that run for hours at a time, and the heart so strong it provides strength to leap fallen logs, bound through ponds, twist through stands of timber and break into a clearing to stalk a herd of elk. The pack will eat once again. The eyes of the wolf are the eyes of survival.

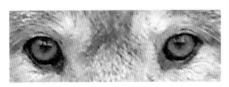

Look into the eyes of dogs. Some sparkle with mischief, some are soft and gentle, others are intense. These eyes don't reflect the wildness of the wolf. They tell us, instead, what the dog has become even while keeping gifts inherited from the wolf.

How the Domestic Dog Came to Be

Before the end of the Pleistocene Epoch and the Ice Age, 12,000 to 15,000 years ago, it was inevitable that wolves and humans would have met at times. Their hunting and scavenging were similar. A few wolves would have stayed relatively close to human camps, eating what food scraps they could find. When a litter was born, some pups would stay close to the human camp while others would return to the wild. This would

> **The dogs we know and love still have "wolfness" in them, even after thousands of years.**

WOLF VERSUS DOG

PHYSICAL DIFFERENCES BETWEEN WOLVES AND DOGS
- The dog has:
  a smaller body size (with exception of giant breeds like the Great Dane),
  shorter muzzle,
  smaller teeth, often crowded,
  shorter and wider skull (which humans bred into bulldog-type breeds),
  or a longer and narrower skull (greyhound-type breeds).
- Most dogs carry their tails curled over the back or in a sickle shape.
- The wolf's tail hangs down.

BEHAVIOR DIFFERENCES BETWEEN WOLVES AND DOGS
- Barking absent in wolves except when they are puppies, common in dogs.
- Trainability weak in wolves, strong in dogs.
- Dominance is complex, follows a line of order in the wolf pack, but varies in different dog breeds.
- Face licking (greeting) common but not often repeated in the wolf, common and often repeated in the dog.

have been the beginning of the process of domestication.

Over time, interaction between humans and wolves led to the development of the dog. By 10,000 years ago humans had domesticated plants such as barley and others, especially those with seeds. Humans became farmers as well as hunters and lived in villages. Small individual dumps and community dumps had a variety of garbage. The appearance of bones of smaller dogs in archeological digs indicates that the smaller wolves, ancestor of these dogs, had been accepted by humans, possibly because these wolves were less frightening than the much larger wolves with their big teeth.

These early dogs were comfortable around humans, and humans accepted them.

Farmers and townspeople began to teach dogs to perform jobs that would aid them in their work. These were herding (sheep were domesticated 11,000 years ago), guarding the sheep from predators, guarding the shopkeepers' wares, and pulling carts for farmers as well as shopkeepers. Other dogs were selected to go with hunters to hunt field birds, rabbits and larger animals.

The improvements of skills, inventions, and arts and symbols of the different cultures continued to progress through the generations. The dog was alongside the humans, being taught the many ways he could assist.

THE WHEN AND WHERE OF THE FIRST DOGS

Early discoveries of dogs with humans were made by archeologists. These are scientists who study the

One of the oldest is a jaw bone dated 14,000 years ago.

THE FOX EXPERIMENT

Dogs are descended from wolves. It isn't easy to think of the Pomeranian, the Poodle, or the Bassett Hound as having almost the same genetic structure as the wolf (98%). How did this come about?

Some of the best evidence about the origin of the dog from the wolf comes from an experiment in Russia. In the 1950s, a geneticist, Dmitry Belyaev, worked with a colony of wild foxes on a fur farm in Siberia. The purpose of the experiment was to develop wild foxes that would be easier for the employees to handle and care for. Belyaev and his partner, Ludmila N. Trut, believed that a calmer temperament could be inherited if the foxes in the breeding program were selected carefully.

The study contained 465 foxes. Belyaev selected the more quiet foxes, that were still too wild to handle, for the study.

After eighteen generations of selecting the least wild of the foxes for breeding, a great change occurred. Foxes that wanted to be around people appeared. They behaved like dogs, licking hands and faces, jumping up, wagging their tails vigorously and barking excitedly. These foxes had been selected and bred to have a good attitude toward people.

In the process, however, their appearance changed. The original silver gray color was now mottled brown and gray with occasional large white spots. Other dog-like changes included a turned up tail and floppy ears, not fox-like at all.

This relates to those wolves thirty thousand years ago who stayed close to the campfires. As the generations of breeding went on, the wolf-dogs became calmer and friendlier around people, less like wolves and more like domesticated wolves which became known as dogs. Different looking breeds developed during the following thousands of years when people began to select for specific characteristics that they wanted for their own purposes.

remains of the culture of a people. They use carbon dating to determine the age of their findings. One of the

This American Timber Wolf is displaying the intense eyes and posture of a prey animal stalking its victim.

oldest of these is a jaw bone of a domestic dog in Germany found in 1979 in a grave at Oberkassel and dated to 14,000 years before the present. Another find was from a site named Ein Mallaha in the upper Jordan valley in Israel dated 12,000 years ago; its inhabitants are called Natufians. It was a skeleton in a tomb of an elderly human lying on its side, legs flexed, with its hand resting on the chest of a four- or five-month old domestic dog puppy. Many dog bones and teeth demonstrating a wide range of size and body shapes have been found in Middle East digs, and artifacts of dog bones continue to be discovered in all parts of the world.

Strong evidence found by researchers in the science of genetics has shown that most dogs are descended from the Grey Wolf. How do they know this? Because of the discovery and use of mitochondrial DNA (mtDNA), a discovery that pushed the research further back in time. It is passed from generation to generation like other DNA, but only through the mother. As it was passed on to every puppy in every litter, it carried the genetic qualities of the wolf during the thousands of years in which the dog became the domesticated wolf, a species of its own. By sequence analysis of mtDNA, the trail can be followed. (See mtDNA sidebar.)

Recent studies offer some of the first genetic evidence of the when and

Mitochondria are the power plants of our cells. They convert food into energy within the cells that the body uses for all its functions such as heart, lungs and eyes. They are located inside the cell wall but not in the nucleus. mtDNA have their own DNA material. But unlike the DNA in the cell's nucleus which comes from both parents, mtDNA is passed down from the mother dog to all females in a litter of puppies. They in turn pass it on to all females in their litters. Researchers can trace maternal lineage far back in time with mtDNA. This makes it possible to trace the early history of the dog. (See also the definition in the Glossary.)

where of the origin of the dog. Peter Savolainen of Sweden's Royal Institute of Technology examined 654 dogs representing all major dog populations of the world, including those south of the Yangtze River which had not been included in other studies. More than ninety-five percent of the dogs belonged to just three major mtDNA groups carried by females and had as a common ancestor the Grey Wolf.

The greatest differences in the sequences turned up in samples from East Asia, which meant that dogs had been domesticated there the longest. The domestic dog, Savolainen concluded, probably developed in East Asia, perhaps as recently as 15,000 years ago, spread across Asia and Europe, and then traveled to the New World with migrating groups of humans.

A research team led by Bridgett M. von Holdt and Robert K. Wayne of the University of California, Los Angeles, analyzed a large number of wolf and dog DNA. Dr. Wayne collected wolf DNA over many years from wolf packs around the world. A colleague, Elaine Ostran-

der, gathered much of the dog DNA by persuading owners at dog shows to let her take a scraping of cells from inside the cheek. They found that the Middle East was where dog and wolf DNA were most similar, although there was an overlap with the study between East Asian wolves and dogs. The researchers concluded that after dogs were domesticated in the Middle East they spread to East Asia and some cross-breeding put more wolf genes into the dog DNA.

The study by Jennifer Leonard of the Smithsonian Institute and Carlos Vila showed that dogs in the New World also "shared a common origin from Old World grey wolves." Most scientists agree that a wild wolf is genetically no more distant from a domestic dog than a wild mustang is from a horse.

This is an exciting time in the research into the natural history of the dog with more publications about how dogs immigrated to all parts of the world and how the environment affected their appearance and the work they were bred to do.

PARIAH DOG populations of the world differ greatly from modern specialized breeds. They differ in structure and skull shape, in behavior, and also genetically. In fact, mtDNA studies indicate that Asian/Pacific dogs, Basenjis and Dingoes are more closely related to one another and to pariah and primitive dog populations around the globe than to other modern breeds. Some researchers indicate that the pariah dog traces back to the Chinese wolf, a sub-species of the canis lupus, now extinct.

Pariah dogs live in a semi-wild state in Africa, Australia and other remote regions of the world. These wild Dingos live in Australia.

Pariah dogs, which still exist in Africa, Australia, the Middle East, some populated South Pacific islands, and South and Central America, as well as on Native American reservations, shed further light on the development of the dog. Pariahs are dogs of great antiquity. They have been uncovered in archaeological digs in Africa dating back to the Iron Age. They live on the fringes of human society and the true pariah remains a generalized type of dog recognizable over much of the globe and over time. Dogs whose remains have been uncovered by archaeologists in ancient Egypt are much the same as those that scavenge around rural Africa today.

Many pariahs are village and street dogs. They are neither mongrels nor strays and don't belong to anyone. They are around people in the routine of daily life and have a friendly attitude. They don't care to be petted and people accept them as they are. Sometimes food is left out for them; there is always the garbage dump. They are usually medium size, with a smaller head than a wolf, short hair and similar colors, either brown or black. (But in some locations other colors exist. There must have been an outside visitor.) These dogs are very likely to be descendants of the original dogs. They have found their niche on the planet.

The Development of Different Breeds

Many researchers believe that at least four major types of dogs evolved from the original wolf-dog ancestors: the mastiff type, the sight hound, the northern breeds, and the sheepdog. From these four major types, breeds were developed through selective breeding and by crossbreeding among the four types.

The first evidence of distinct breeds of dogs dates back 3,000 years to Egypt and Mesopotamia (an area between the Tigris and Euphrates rivers). The Greyhound is considered to be the foundation of the sight hounds with their narrow head, light body and long legs. This recognizable shape has been found in art, pottery and in tombs. Other breeds of this general type are the Ibizan Hound, the Pharaoh Hound and the Saluki. These breeds, favorites of the pharaohs and royalty, were used for their speed in hunting hare and occasionally the gazelle. They have the sharpest eyes in the dog world.

China was home to many ancient breeds. A sculptural form has been discovered that dates the Chow Chow back to two thousand years ago. Due to the fact that Chinese emperors destroyed the art and literature of their predecessors, most of the evidence of the early development of many breeds is missing. However, the history of

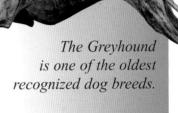

The Greyhound is one of the oldest recognized dog breeds.

The Japanese Chin is one of the oldest toy breeds.

Imagine what the ancient grey wolf would think if he could see all the different dogs that are in his family tree.

The stately Wolfhound was bred to hunt and kill wolves. An Irish Wolfhound is reported to have traveled with Columbus on his fourth voyage to America to become the first purebred dog in the New World.

breeds of the Far East such as the Pekingese, Japanese Chin, Shiba Inu, Tibetan Spaniel and the Pug makes interesting reading. The Akita, also an ancient breed, was designated as one of Japan's national treasures by the Japanese government in 1931.

By the Roman period, 500 B.C. to 395 A.D., most of the main breed types were defined, and their body types and working abilities were recorded. Hunting dogs, guard dogs, and lap dogs were common. Guard

Bird dogs such as retrievers and pointers were developed to assist their owners while hunting waterfowl and game birds.

dogs of the mastiff type were used in battle. Even at that time the Romans understood that selecting dogs to breed for their appearance also affected the resulting behavior and working ability.

The greatest period for the increase of dog breeds in Europe was the Middle Ages, from the 13th to the 15th centuries. This was the era of feudalism, when hunting was the ultimate symbol of power and status to the aristocracy. Different breeds of dogs were developed for the various kinds of hunting. These included Deerhounds, Wolfhounds, Boarhounds and Otterhounds.

In the 18th and 19th centuries during the Industrial Revolution, a middle class developed in England. Although many new jobs paid little and kept people in poverty, other people benefited from the job growth and were able to afford to keep dogs as pets. At the same time, the wealthy class began to develop dog breeds. Breeders who had large kennels with many dogs began to select for the characteristics they wanted, such as the shapes of ears, muzzles, and tails, as well as natural abilities. The breeds that resulted include Foxhounds, Retrievers, Irish Setters, the Spaniels, Terriers, and English Pointers, to name a few. The dog breeds we see most often today were developed in Great Britain and Europe during this time and on into the 20th century.

During this same period, the 18th and 19th centuries, Native American dogs

Terriers were bred to hunt small game like mice and ground squirrel, but they love to play games, too.

Sled dogs love to work pulling sleds.

were companions and guard dogs for the Indian tribes. European travelers wrote that the native dogs would attack them and had to be driven off with sticks and stones. Dogs of the Plains Tribes were an assortment of sizes and colors, and were hard workers when it was time to move the camp. They would be loaded with packs containing tents, kettles and

PUREBRED DOGS

Purebred dogs are members of a recognized breed which has not been mixed with any other dog over many generations. There are well over 600 known breeds worldwide.

Two and three hundred years ago the number of people interested in developing specific breeds grew rapidly in Europe and Great Britain. These breeders were among the wealthy who could afford to maintain a large number of dogs while they developed a breed to fit their needs. When these breeders were satisfied with the appearance and natural ability they wanted, they gave their breed a name and formed a registry. After that, no further mixing with other breeds was allowed. Breed registries and kennel clubs have been formed to maintain those records in most developed countries of the world.

The American Kennel Club (AKC), organized in 1884, acts as a registry for purebred dogs in the United States and maintains breeding and competition records. The United Kennel Club (UKC) also registers many breeds and sponsors dog shows, obedience trials and performance tests. Dog shows are a great way to observe many different breeds. Several national dog shows, such as the Westminster Show in February, appear on television.

firewood. Dogs trained for this job were very docile even when puppies and children ran in, out, and around them. They just kept walking all day in the heat or cold.

Other Plains Indians relied on the travois, two poles crossed over the dog's shoulders, which worked well in flat country. Navajo and Hopi tribes in the Southwest used herding dogs which they acquired from the Spanish explorers.

In the Arctic, husky-type dogs pulling sleds were the only means of transportation until the 1960s when snowmobiles became available. These dogs probably originated in Russia and migrated to North America.

THE DOGS WE KNOW TODAY

Dogs as we know them now have become companions and helpers in ways humans have selected for over many centuries. Dogs choose to live with people. They want to please their people. They no longer want to return to the wild.

Even though dogs no longer have the skills to survive in the wild, they still have remnants of wolf instincts. We need to understand what these are and how they affect a dog's behavior. If we don't accept a dog *as a dog*, if we don't understand what makes him act like a dog, then we won't be able to teach him how to live peacefully in the world of people.

When trained and understood, dogs have much to offer us. They do jobs: guide blind people, help handicapped people in wheelchairs, alert deaf people to

MIXED BREED DOGS

Mixed Breeds or mutts, as they are also called, continue to comprise a large percentage of family pets. They were almost the only dogs seen in small towns and neighborhoods of cities. In the years following World War II, purebreds became more numerous as more people could afford them. Nevertheless, mutts maintained their position as family dog. Mutts have a variety of talents and are loved for what they are.

Another type of mixed breed dogs is called designer dogs or hybrid dogs. They are a combination of two purebred dogs, each parent being a different breed. An example of this is a Labradoodle, a combination of a Labrador Retriever and a Standard Poodle. Other breeds are being used in combinations to produce these hybrid puppies. Time will tell how they fit into the dog world.

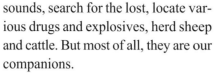

sounds, search for the lost, locate various drugs and explosives, herd sheep and cattle. But most of all, they are our companions.

A lot of people expect their dog to behave like a little person in a fur coat. But by the time a puppy is six months old and begins to follow its instincts and act like a dog—chewing everything, pulling on the leash, and taking food off the kitchen counter—the puppy's people don't know what to do. They don't understand that dogs must be taught how to live with people, and that dog owners need to learn how to live with their dogs.

Humans and dogs have lived together for so long that our dogs have become very sensitive to us, even though we aren't necessarily tuned in to what's going on with them. But can we know the dog's thoughts? No. The dog is not from human ancestry. We are not from canine ancestry. The wolf is the species *Canis lupus*. The dog is the species *Canis familiarus*. We are the species *Homo sapiens*. These species are unrelated, two very different species on the same planet. That we can live togeth-

Dogs choose to live with people. They want to please their people. They no longer want to return to the wild.

er and experience many of each other's feelings is one of the amazements of our lives on planet earth.

Does a puppy or a dog know how he should behave when he comes to live with us in our house? Of course not. Dogs don't have a clue about what we want them to do or not do until we show them.

While we can't know what a dog is thinking, we can learn what makes him behave the way he does. When you know this you will better understand "dog-speak," a unique and wonderful language. Your dog will be happy now that you understand him, and you will become true partners.

chapter three

CORKY'S INSTINCTS AND SENSES

All during the centuries when the dog was little understood by humans, dogs were watching us, learning to adapt to us. They know the signs of our moods and illnesses by the expression in our eyes. They understand our body language when we sprain an ankle or

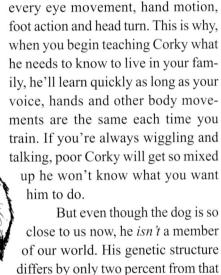

have a stomachache. They notice every eye movement, hand motion, foot action and head turn. This is why, when you begin teaching Corky what he needs to know to live in your family, he'll learn quickly as long as your voice, hands and other body movements are the same each time you train. If you're always wiggling and talking, poor Corky will get so mixed up he won't know what you want him to do.

But even though the dog is so close to us now, he *isn't* a member of our world. His genetic structure differs by only two percent from that of the wolf. He has adapted to humans and chooses to live in our world, but the dogs we know and love still have "wolfness" in them, even after thousands of years.

Because of this ancestry, the puppy is an immigrant in our

Instincts influence a dog's behavior, and his senses give him amazing abilities.

world. Like any immigrant, he wants to be part of this new world, which to him means being part of his people pack. So he joins his human pack ready and eager to learn about his new culture—but he brings along his wolf instincts.

DOGS BEHAVE BY INSTINCT

Dogs operate from instincts which are inherited from their wolf ancestors or which were bred into a certain breed or type of dog through generations of selecting for certain characteristics. Each of the instincts listed below is part of a dog's personality. To us, these instincts are the qualities that make the dog fun or helpful to have in the family.

The HUNTING instinct, (locating prey), uses the dog's keen sense of sight or smell and can be used in many ways to assist his human friends.

The PREY instinct, one of the most powerful instincts, has a specific role—to chase and capture prey. In the family, it activates the dog to retrieve and to play games.

The PACK instinct is what makes your dog want to live with us in our people pack.

The HERDING instinct keeps the dog alert and on duty to keep track of the family members.

The GUARDING instinct triggers the dog to let the family know when someone approaches the house.

The COMMUNICATION instinct directs your dog to communicate through his body language and to be aware of non-verbal communication, such as when Corky seems to sense when you're sad or worried or sick.

Every dog carries all of these instincts to a lesser or greater degree. For example, some breeds such as Border Collies and Welsh Corgis want to herd anything that moves, even if it's only their family in the back yard. Other breeds such as the Australian Terrier and the Standard Poodle rarely show any desire to herd any kind of critter. They have a low herding instinct because the people who breed these dogs have selected for other abilities. The Australian Terrier helped control rodents and snakes, and the Standard Poodle was originally a water retriever. But all breeds of dogs still have some herding instinct that will show up under certain conditions.

The Prey Instinct

The wolf is a hunter. The prey instinct governs his life. He lives for his major reward, to locate food, chase it and kill it. The instinct to hunt is ever present, always turned on, ready to activate.

The dog is a hunter, too. The prey instinct is in all dogs, usually to a milder degree than in the wolf. Many

A Border Collie herding sheep.

dogs that live sheltered lives seldom have an opportunity to display prey behavior except perhaps for pouncing on a toy or chasing after a ball. But even for dogs that rarely leave home, certain sounds and movements can activate the prey instinct and cause the dog to react like a wolf.

Chasing a cat or a squirrel relates to the prey instinct. Teasing a dog to get him excited, "Get that cat, get it, get it," can increase a mild prey instinct to the point that the dog becomes a cat killer. Occasionally dogs that don't live in a city, when let loose outside at night, will injure or kill a sheep, chicken, or pet rabbit. Two dogs together can become a pack. If one of them has a strong prey instinct, he will lead the other to hunt for an animal to attack.

Another example of prey instinct involves children who are running and playing. The sounds of laughing or shouting in high-pitched voices can excite dogs, triggering the prey instinct and causing some dogs to chase and jump on the children. Even a small dog can cause injury by scratching legs or biting at the leg or ankle. The erratic motions of a toddler walking or running can look like a small animal, and a dog could bump and knock the child down.

Dogs must be taught that they can't behave this way. The dog is an intelligent animal capable of learning what actions are not acceptable. Corky can learn to resist his prey instinct. (See Chapter 7 for details.)

Let Corky Go On A Virtual Hunt

If a dog is never allowed to participate in prey-drive activities he can become over-active, easily excitable, or impatient. He might even over-react with slight provocation and bite or chase. If he's frustrated, he will probably substitute such actions as fence running in the yard or barking constantly. Have you ever noticed how on a walk a dog sniffs different scents in the grass or around trees? He comes home in a calm state of mind, often sleeping and woofing and moving his legs like he's running, because he's had vigorous exercise, and also because he has used his hunting instinct.

You can quite easily let Corky experience the prey instinct. To a dog, this means new sights and smells, being part of a group, and being out in nature. It can be as simple as going on a walk, a jog on a woodland or greenbelt trail, a game of fetch, a leap for a Frisbee, a reward of food for a job well done, or a ride in the car and going places with the family.

The energy of dogs who have a strong prey instinct can be defused with games.

Let Corky sniff. SNIFFING is a dog's way of learning about the world he lives in. Smell is as important to a dog as seeing is to us. It's part of being a dog.

- Taking a dog for a walk or a jog might exercise him, but if you don't stop at places like trees and fire plugs and take time to let him sniff around, you've given him nothing to do that is a part of the dog's world. You can do him a favor by taking him on leash to the park or around the neighborhood. (*Remember your plastic bag to clean up after your dog.*)
- If it's a slow walk because he finds things to sniff, be patient. Give him a few minutes, and then tell him it's time to move on, hunting in a different area. This is your gift to him to keep him relaxed in a people's world.
- A good walk you will both enjoy combines slow and brisk walking. Remember, you are in charge.
- Whenever possible take Corky with your family to a different place and let him sniff. This imitates hunting, and you couldn't give him a better gift.

Another way to let him express his prey instinct is by playing retrieving games with you. The energy of dogs who have a strong prey instinct, such as Retrievers and Terriers (and individuals in other breeds, too), can be defused with these games. (For further details refer to Chapter 8.)

Playing Frisbee is one way a dog expresses the prey instinct.

All of these activities help the dog release the restlessness he would have if he could never use basic actions related to his prey instinct because he never leaves the back yard. No matter how comfy Corky's life is, we will never be able to take the prey instinct totally out of his mind or his behavior, and we probably don't want to. It is a part of his natural being. Helping him express this in acceptable ways helps us, too. We are working with him in our world, allowing him to keep his dogness (instincts) but to use acceptable ways to express them.

THE DOG'S REMARKABLE SENSES

With their keen senses, dogs behave and perceive in ways we humans can only marvel at. Their finely tuned noses, their ears, and their sharp eyesight, all adapted to the jobs they were bred to do, contribute to making the dog a being with very special gifts.

The Nose Knows: Scenting Defines His World

Dogs live in a world of odors. Their sense of smell is their most refined sense. Dogs have inherited this ability from the wolf.

Wherever they are, in the neighborhood, across town, to the park and back home again, dogs, like wolves, "see" with their noses. One sniff tells the wolf a lot: who was there and how long ago they went by (even weeks). It can tell the sex of the others and what their position in the social order is.

With their noses, dogs identify friends, strangers, good guys and bad guys. Their scenting ability opens to them a world we know nothing about. When they are scenting in the outdoors they are in the world of the wild. We can

Dogs explore the world with their noses. This Akita is checking out a Bichon Frise that in turn is sniffing the scent of something in the grass.

A German Shepherd police dog checks luggage for drugs or explosives.

teach them what we want them to find, but once they begin, whether ground scenting or air scenting, they function on their own. In that world they are far superior to their human pack members. Their scenting (olfactory) ability makes them valuable in identifying drugs, explosives, and people in collapsed buildings or buried in avalanches and in searching for lost children and hikers.

The scent membrane inside a dog's nose is about four times greater in area than the same membrane in humans. In the dog's nose there are over 200 million scent receptors in the

SEAL-SNIFFING DOGS

In the frozen lands of the north, scientists are studying ringed seals to learn about their breeding sites and numbers—when they can find them. A person can walk along on top of the snow and see no signs of the seals.

Enter the Labrador Retriever. Though not the first dogs to sniff out seals, (the Inuit Indians used dogs for this a long time ago), they are now helping the scientists with a tagging project. When the snow gets deep enough, the seals create snow caves for breeding, with small breathing holes through cracks in the ice. Dogs can smell the seal holes under the snow.

The Labradors run ahead of the snowmobiles, running in a zigzag pattern when they get a whiff of seal. The researchers call them off from digging and set up a capture net in the bottom of the hole. The scientists return to their huts. When the seal swims up to the hole, it triggers a radio signal. With a remote trigger, the scientists quickly close the net, get on their snowmobiles and ride to the hole. They sweep off the snow, grab the seal and tag it. They collect DNA from sealskin specks left on the ice.

One project takes place in Pearl Bay and Point Barrow in northeastern Alaska, more than 300 miles north of the Artic Circle. Of concern to the researchers is an increasingly early snowmelt. The lives of the seal pups depend upon staying in the snow caves with their mothers for two months after birth; early snowmelts mean they could freeze to death.

The researchers first tried using an infrared camera that detects body heat, but they could detect seal holes only if the dogs first showed them where they were. The seal-sniffing dogs have greater than an eighty percent success rate.

nasal folds compared to our 5 million. Moisture on the nose helps to capture scent and transmit it onto odor-sensitive nasal membranes.

Dogs can move one nostril at a time which lets them sense the direction from which a scent is coming. In a dog's nasal passage there is a kind of shelf. When a dog sniffs, the sense molecules go up over the shelf where they can accumulate. When a dog pants the air passes below the shelf. The dog's receptors sort through the different scent molecules and then send electrical signals to the brain. Two structures in the lower part of the brain sort out all the different scents and the information they carry. These structures are called olfactory nodules and a dog's are about four times larger than a humans.

Humans tend to smell one scent at a time but a dog can sort through many scents that occur at the same time, separating them and responding to each one mentally. If a dog is at a picnic and his nose brings in the scents of hot dogs, potato salad, marshmallows, chocolate bars and graham crack-ers, and a rotten fish 100 feet down the shore, his brain processes them at the same time, and the fish wins. Another dog might choose the hot dogs, and another the sweet marshmallows.

Taste Doesn't Work Alone

When it comes to taste, most of it has to do with the smell. When a dog takes a bite, the aroma goes from the back of the mouth to the nasal passages and on to the brain. The influence of smell mostly covers the taste. This limits the possibilities for research on taste in dogs because it's almost impossible to isolate taste from smell.

Some facts are known. The number of taste buds is estimated from 1,700 to 2,000, compared to about 10,000 for humans. Much of this difference might be made up

> **Perhaps dogs have a genetic memory of many of the poisonous plants.**

by the dog's superior scenting ability. The taste buds are mostly in the front of the mouth on the tongue. The food or item sends sensations to the brain. It notes five different flavors, salty, sour, sweet, bitter, and Unami, which is monosodium glutamate, newly recognized as a flavor. It occurs in nature and foods containing proteins, such as milk, meat, peas and some cheeses.

Most dogs don't like a bitter taste. Most toxins, poisons, in nature are bitter. Perhaps dogs have a genetic memory of many of these poisonous plants. Dogs don't always eat something because they like the taste. They eat because it's there: garbage, a bag of candy or a sandwich on the counter. This goes back to their history of being scavengers, grabbing whatever it is as fast as they can before another wolf or dog got it.

If you want the best-tasting food for your dog, let him tell you. If he starts eating as soon as you give it to him, he likes it. You want quality ingredients in the food. Ask your veterinarian or a friend who knows dog foods for advice.

The Sense of Touch

When we touch a dog we receive pleasure from stroking his coat. But what does touch mean to a dog? Touch is the first sense a puppy develops. The mother dog begins touching newborn puppies almost immediately after birth by licking and nuzzling, encouraging each new puppy to eat. The senses of sight and hearing are not active yet. The puppy learns about his environment through touch. You can observe him crawling around moving his head from side to side until he bumps into his mother or a littermate. Throughout the pup's first weeks, the mother's touching with her tongue and her body and the contact with littermates are very important to the dog's mental maturity. People who raise a litter in their home know the value of picking up each puppy every day and stroking him gently. If a puppy gets no touching from humans he turns out to be fearful and inattentive.

Dogs love to be scratched behind the ear, or patted on the chest. They love to be scratched at the base of the tail, stroked along the neck and along the side, and, of course, rubbed on the tummy. Most dogs prefer a gentle to medium level of touch. Few choose a hard or too rapid level. A dog should be touched every day, no special amount of time, no special place, just a hand on that special furry body.

Dogs don't like to be touched in some places. Being patted on top of the head is unpleasant for some. He lets you know this by turning his head or moving away. Other dogs have families who do this and they don't

A dog should be touched every day.

mind. Almost all dogs don't like to be hugged and will try to get away from the hugger. The space between toes is especially sensitive and many dogs don't want their feet touched. To help a dog accept having his feet touched, distract him with a treat while handling his feet. Begin slowly and as the dog gets used to having his feet held for a short time, gradually increase the time. Don't hold on to a dog's feet any longer than he will allow. By touching the dog's feet every day he will let them be handled. This is important because dogs need their nails trimmed, and in wet weather should allow their feet to be dried or mud wiped off before entering the house. With the exception of the feet, respect their feelings when they try to tell you a certain touch isn't a good one for them.

How does a dog feel touches? The feel of being touched is determined by the touch receptors at the base of the hair follicles. Some areas of the dog's body are more sensitive to touch than others. This is related to the higher or lower number of touch receptors in that area. A very sensitive area is the upper and lower jaw and the whiskers, known as vibrissae. They are stiffer and longer than other hairs and each one has more touch receptors at its base than anywhere else. Dogs use these hairs to learn more about their environment. Whiskers are sensitive to vibrations and slight movements of air currents and inform the dog that something is getting close to his face. This avoids a collision whether it's a wall, another dog or a person. Some breeders of show dogs trimmed off the whiskers for dog shows, but when they learned that whiskers were important the practice largely ceased.

How do dogs touch? With their nose, paws and tongue, of course. With the nose, it's a push under the arm of a person who is sitting, even trying to lift the hand to encourage petting. If the person is standing, the dog will position his muzzle or head directly under the hand if it is within reach. The nose can get pushy. The paw is used in the same way, only more gently. It's almost like a motion that says, "Here I am." We all know what the tongue does. It slurps, or is a delicate lick from a small tongue. The message? "I'm so happy to see you."

People love to touch dogs. Dogs love to touch people, each in their own way.

His Ears Hear What We Cannot

If a dog is part of your family pack you already know how sharp his hearing is. As stealthily as you try, you can't begin to open a bag of a snack package without having your dog appear from wherever he was in the house.

The biggest difference in the hearing of dogs and humans is in the high frequency range. Young humans can hear frequencies up to 12,000 Hertz. As they get older, they lose the ability to hear some of the highest tones. A Hertz (Hz) is a measure of sound in wavelength or cycles per second. Human ears are tuned to the sounds that are most important to them. Frequencies between 500 and 4,000 Hz are the best for hearing speech. The top quality (sensitivity) of hearing is at

DEAFNESS IN DOGS

Deafness occurs in dogs of any breed or mixed breeds. Some dogs are born deaf. Others can't hear as a result of an accident or disease such as a bacterial or fungal infection. Deaf dogs can lead a nearly normal life using their eyes and nose. Most deaf dogs learn hand signals readily. These dogs need protection and should be kept in the house or on a leash at all times. They can't hear cars or children playing or a person they don't see who reaches out to pet them. This can startle them severely and they could react by snapping or biting at the source of the touch.

If you want to test your dog's hearing, get behind him so that he can't see you and squeeze a squeaky toy, bang a spoon against a pan, or blow a whistle. Your dog should turn toward you or move his ears or turn his head. But just because your dog doesn't come when he's called does not mean he can't hear. Trainers call this "selective hearing." The dog chooses NOT to hear you. It's time for more training.

Some dogs are overly sensitive to high frequency tones. This is why common sounds from vacuum sweepers, lawn mowers, blenders, or some power tools can be painful to dogs—they may have intense shrieks to dogs that people cannot hear.

2,000 Hz. This compares to the maximum sensitivity of a dog that is tuned much higher, at about 8,000 Hz.

Dogs can hear much higher-pitched sounds than people. The highest ranges are between 47,000 and 65,000 Hz. They can hear at this range as a result of the evolutionary development of their wolf ancestors. In the winter their diet was big game such as deer, elk and moose, which they hunted in packs. Their summer diet consisted of small rodents such as mice, voles and rats (and it still does). The wolves who could hear the prey's high-pitched sounds and find them were the ones that survived. They had genetically inherited this high-frequency hearing and passed it on to their puppies. Over thousands of years it has become part of the dog's heritage.

The silent whistle was invented to give commands to dogs at a high frequency so that humans couldn't hear them. After dogs are trained, police and protection agencies give commands with the whistles that tell the dogs to stop or corner a suspect.

How Dogs See the World

Most dogs have eyesight of 20/70, compared to the perfect sight for humans of 20/20. This means that a dog must be as close as 20 feet to see as well as a person with 20/20 vision sees at 75 feet.

Although vision is not the dog's strongest sense, it works well when the object is in motion. Movement of a ball or Frisbee, or a running squirrel or cat, attracts a dog's atention. That is why a rabbit will freeze to avoid being found. Many dogs won't see it even if it is in open ground. Once the dog wanders closer the rabbit starts to run; the dog sees it, and the chase begins.

Some dogs see better than others. A Labrador Retriever can see a duck flying over a river 200 to 300 yards away—two or three football fields' distance. (A football field is 100 yards long.) As the duck gets closer and is shot, the Retriever marks where it falls, goes straight to it and then uses his nose to zero in.

The Saluki, Greyhound and Ibizan are ancient breeds developed in Egypt, Arabia and other Middle Eastern countries. Their remarkable sight and speed gave them advantages in the wide vistas of desert country. These sight hounds could see an animal, a rabbit or gazelle, moving in the far distance and either chase and catch it or lead their humans to the animal.

Most dogs' eyes have a large black pupil. It gathers light into the eye and the larger the pupil the more light it collects. This lets in

SMALL BREEDS such as Pugs, Yorkshire Terriers and Shih Tzu have three times as many nerve endings in the retinas of their eyes as do the hunting breeds. The toy breeds see more like humans but in more detail. This helps them see changes in their person's facial expression, and is probably the reason toy dogs are so affectionate and like to stay close to people.

a lot of whatever light is available during the darker times of the day. Dogs see better than humans in the evening and early morning and can also see better than humans at night. This is an inheritance from the wolf and is not as important to companion dogs in our communities who are mostly out during the day, but is valuable for guard dogs and dogs who work with policemen.

Most dogs have some binocular vision (like humans who don't need glasses), but their lack of a full binocular vision is offset by a wider side vision. In most dogs the eyes are set wider apart than human eyes, which gives them a much wider range of area.

In low light conditions a dog's vision is improved by a special reflecting surface, called the tapetum lucidum, located behind the retina. The pupil dilates, allowing as much light as possible to enter the eye. Unabsorbed light passing over the retina is concentrated on the tapetum and reflected back over the light sensitive rods. This creates a greater sensation of light to maintain vision beyond what humans can see after the sun goes down.

Dogs evolved as night hunters and scavengers. Their eyes have a different number of nerve cells, known as rods and cones, than humans have. Dogs have more light-sensitive rods to see better at dusk and dawn. Their eyes have two color-sensitive cones, versus three in humans, so they see fewer colors than we do. They see dark blue, light blue, gray, light yellow (almost brown), dark yellow and very dark gray, but they see blues and yellows best. The colors that we can see are various shades of gray to a dog. A dog might run past a red ball on the grass because it wasn't as visible as a blue ball. Sometimes a bright contrast with the background or the shininess of the object can make objects easier to see.

When it comes to seeing people they know, dogs begin to recognize them first by their walk or certain body movements. As the person gets closer, the dog uses his nose to verify who it is. This is when he gets excited.

These natural abilities are part of what makes the dog so special.

chapter four

HOW DOGS LEARN TO LIVE WITH PEOPLE

The first sixteen weeks are the most important time in a puppy's life. The puppy's instincts and sensory abilities are all developing at different times in the first few weeks and months. At the same time another need is beginning that will affect his behavior the rest of his life. One of his basic instincts is to live in a pack (his human pack) and to know how to act around other dogs. This is called socialization. It is a learning process. The lack of this leads a dog to a life of frustration because he is either fearful or aggressive to other dogs, and some humans, as well. This hinders a normal life of fun with his human family.

The under-socialized dog often becomes fearful of anything new—people, dogs, places, anything. This is shown by excessive barking, anxiety, dog aggression, fear and hyperactivity. The socialized dog is confident around people and other dogs and seldom displays anxiety in new environments. Socialization introduces more learning experiences. The under-socialized dog has a brain that lacks the huge array of neural (brain) connections of the well socialized dog that lives in an enriched environment with toys and home activities.

The dog is born with every brain cell he will ever need for his whole life. But his brain is tiny –a one-day-old puppy has a brain about the size of the tip of an adult person's little finger. Although the wolf's brain is larger, that doesn't mean he's smarter. He needs a bigger brain to survive in the wild. Most of his connections are genetic, which means they are hard-wired. The puppy's brain makes many connections which come from the stimulation of his experiences. Sixteen weeks later, the puppy's brain is

> The first sixteen weeks are the most important time in a puppy's life.

Puppies should be handled and socialized from the time they are very young.

10 times larger than at birth. It grows to almost 80% of its final size during these few weeks.

The increase in the size of the brain comes almost entirely from the number of connections that are made between the cells. These connectors are like pathways or branches that attach many brain cells. Millions of connections between tens of millions of brain cells occur from the experiences a puppy has during his first 16 weeks. Just the way a tree keeps growing more and more branches as it matures, a puppy's brain keeps making these vital connections. Many of these cell connections occur automatically when the pup receives the genetic signals for walking, eating, hearing, seeing, and all the other physical functions, but others come from what he encounters in daily life with his people.

THOSE NEURONS (BRAIN CELLS) KEEP COMMUNICATING

When the connecting pathways between brain cells have been developed, one brain cell can send different messages to thousands of other cells, which give the dog the ability to learn many activities: retrieving the newspaper, announcing visitors, playing games, performing tricks and being a special companion. The more connections that exist between brain cells, the easier it will be for the pup to learn to adjust to changes he might meet later in his life: a new home, new people, and different dogs.

Much of this wiring happens when the pup is exposed to many sights, smells, and sounds, plays with toys, is with people, goes on walks, meets other dogs and goes places with the family. These con-

> **A wagging tail is a good sign of socialization.**

nections involve future behavior, and problem-solving skills that a dog develops as he matures come from the many experiences he has in his first 16 weeks. The cells that aren't used begin to wither away. The puppy who never goes any place and is seldom played with will have a smaller brain and won't have the same learning potential as the puppy who has had many experiences.

Many people want to adopt an adult dog, and this is a good thing. Often, there is no way of knowing how much socializing the dog had during his first 16 weeks. But the dog's attitude towards people and other dogs tells what his personality is like. A wagging tail, willingness to approach a new person, and lack of fear are good signs of socialization. Best of all, a socialized dog will calm down after a vigorous play period, rather than stay wound up. On the other hand, the under-socialized dog often becomes fearful of anything new—people, other dogs, places, anything. This is shown by excessive barking, anxiety, aggression, fear and hyperactivity. Training

can improve some of these behaviors, but that takes time, effort and patience.

There are a few dogs, though, that will never fit into a family. These dogs have been too severely abused as puppies, teased too much with a stick, or left isolated and never had the opportunity to socialize. Occasionally, a dog's genetic make-up is the cause.

THE SOCIALIZATION PERIOD

This is the term commonly used for the first 16 weeks. Although the wolf has a socialization period too, it only lasts for 19 days, beginning the day he's born. A large number of the wolf's brain cell connections involve the senses of sight, sound, and hearing, which are necessary for finding food and surviving in the wild. Most of the neuron connections in the wolf happen automatically.

While the wolf's brain is making connections with genetic information that he needs to know to survive in the wild, the dog's brain is making connections from the

Playing with toys is stimulating for puppies. This Labradoodle puppy likes his teddy bear.

new experiences he is having, which will help him know what to do in other new situations.

During the many thousands of years of living near and with humans, the dog's socialization period gradually lengthened to 16 weeks. This can also be called the time of mental agility. The dog's mind is more flexible as a result of a large amount of interaction with his environment and with humans.

The ability to cooperate is also developing during this time. A person can train his dog to obey a command that will interrupt an instinct. For example, if a dog sees a squirrel, his instinct is to chase it, but he can be trained to respond to his person's command and stay with him rather than run. The dog's chase instinct can be overpowered by training and by large amounts of rewards and praise. But this training must start before the dog develops an obsession to chase a ball or a cat and doesn't listen to the command.

KEEP THOSE NEURONS CONNECTING

Physical activities introduce a variety of challenges that increase the number of neuron connections. Help your pup navigate the rungs of a ladder lying on the ground and walk a board about 24 inches wide, one to two feet off the ground. Let him run through a tunnel (from a toy store) or a long box with the ends removed and climb up and down wide stairs.

Mental exercises also stimulate brain cells. Practice makes perfect. Teach him the names of his toys by repeating the name when you play with him. One day he'll surprise you by bringing the toy you ask for. Hide a dog biscuit in the room for your pup to find by sniffing. Let him watch you, then help him by guiding him close to it. After he knows the game, teach him to find a favorite toy.

The best part of having fun with a puppy is that he uses his senses—looking, listening, scenting, touching and tasting (a variety of tidbits keeps his interest high)—and you get to see it happening.

SNIFFING GAMES YOU CAN PLAY

1. Have Corky sit and stay while you hide a favorite toy or treat. Start out by making it easy to find, such as placing it behind an open door. As Corky begins to understand "Find It," make the game more challenging.

2. If you have several doorways down a hall, hide the object behind one of the closed doors and have Corky locate the correct door. Open it and give him the treat or let him play with the toy as a reward.

3. Place four paper cups in a row on the floor or grass. Place a treat under one of the cups. Have Corky find it.

4. Put several different types of treats or food (such as cheese, a dog bone, a bite of meat) on paper plates. Place them in a row and see which one Corky goes to first.

5. Tie a string on a meaty bone. While Corky is out of sight, drag the bone across the grass. Pick it up near the end of your trail and hide it. See if Corky will use his nose to find it.

6. Have a friend hide and ask Corky to find her. Then you can hide and have your friend or parent send Corky to find you.

CAN YOU IDENTIFY THESE WAYS TO SOCIALIZE YOUR DOG?

A. Teach your dog to
_____.

B. Let your dog run thru a
_____.

C. Arrange for your dog
to _____
with other dogs.

D. Take your dog on a
_____.
Expose him to many
different places.

E. Train your dog to
_____ the paper
or other items.

F. Teach _____
like "Hi-5" or "Sit Up."

Find the answers on page 94.

chapter five

THE FAMILY PACK

Have you ever met a dog who doesn't do what he's told? He doesn't come when called, jumps up on family and friends after being told "no," and won't stop barking. Maybe he even growls when you pick up one of his toys. Why does he act this way? It may be because he doesn't have a leader—someone in his family pack he respects, who teaches him how to behave, and who praises him when he does what's expected of him.

THE DOG'S PACK

How do you become the leader? How do you gain your dog's respect? Why can't your dog just be a dog—run and jump and be a free spirit? Why? Because a dog is a dog. He needs to know the limits of how to act within the pack. A lot of his bad behaviors happen because he doesn't know what he can or can't do. He just knows he wants to be part of his pack. He wants to know where he fits in.

How do you know that's what he wants? Because you know that he's a pack animal and the instinct of the wolf for living together in a pack is still strong in the dog. If you didn't know that before, you know it now.

When wolf pups are born they stay in their den with their mother for the first couple of weeks. They gradually come out around the other pack members and by four to five weeks until about 16 weeks they have free run of the den area, seldom being disciplined, even by the male pack leader. By five to six months they are out of control, wrestling vigorously and biting too hard in their excitement. It's time for the adult pack members to teach some manners. All of them participate in teaching the

> Dogs must understand their position within the human group.

pups the way of the wild. In order to be hunters they must learn the rules of the pack.

It's the same in the human pack. The family leader, usually a parent, is in charge of the training. The family leader can be male, female, tall, short, big-voiced or quiet. It's an attitude. The leader knows the rules of the house and enforces them. The other members of the family help teach the puppy or the dog the rules of living with humans. If they don't, the dog won't be allowed to be in the house; he's too unruly to take for a walk, he's out of control when friends come, so he stays in the yard or pen all by himself, which makes him even more wild and out of control.

Wolves live and hunt in packs.

Occasionally a dog is born with a leader personality and thinks he's in charge of the family. Dogs like this will bolt out the door ahead of the family leader, grab food off the kitchen counter, or not let anyone touch their food bowl or toys. These dogs must be taught from an early age that they don't give the orders. They shouldn't be taught with physical force such as hitting, continuous hard jerks on the leash or angry shouting. These actions challenge them to maintain their pack position by ignoring the trainer. Nevertheless, *they must learn the rules of the household.*

Teaching a dog with an independent and dominant personality takes many repetitions of the basics such as "sit," "down," "stay," and "come." The human leader guides the dog to perform these commands by hand motions and rewarding with a tidbit in the hand. When you begin with Corky, he won't understand what you want, but he will learn with practice and patience. He learns that the adult in the family is the leader, and second is the assistant leader. That's you.

This one thinks he's in charge.

REMEMBER:

When Corky knows where he stands in the family, he'll be much happier. You and your family will be, too.

HOW DOES CORKY LEARN THAT YOU'RE THE LEADER?

When you're alone with Corky, *you* are top dog! Tone of voice tells him a lot. Be firm but calm, which isn't always easy, especially when he ignores you. Remember, you're not top sergeant,

Pay attention to me.

TEACH TWO IMPORTANT BASIC COMMANDS

The "Sit" command. Keep your hand and treat close to the nose. Move it back toward his eyes if he needs more help. When he leans his head back, he will sit.

"SIT" is one of the most important commands Corky will learn because it is easy for you to use as a reminder that you're in charge. Tell him to "sit" before you feed him, before you play with him, and before you let him go outside.

Another leadership activity involves combining the **"COME"** command with taking Corky for a walk. (You will learn more about this command in Chapter 7.) When he gets to the end of the leash, call him with "Corky, come," followed by a quick pop on the leash. Run backward a few steps. When Corky reaches you, give him a treat and tell him in a happy voice that he's a "good dog." If you have a retractable-lead, Corky can be 10 or 15 feet away when you call him. Give him a treat just about every time he comes to you. Carry the treats in your pocket or in a pack around your waist.

shouting commands, or a grouch with an angry voice. You're the leader. Your dog must pay attention when you call his name and look at you.

Use Food Rewards

You are the leader. You are the giver of all great and wonderful things. A food reward for a job well done is part of his wolf heritage, when the hunt was rewarded with food or when the adult wolves brought food from the kill to the pups. A food reward acts as a big incentive and the dog learns commands quickly.

TEACH YOUR DOG GOOD HOUSE MANNERS

Establish His Special Place

Corky should have his own special place in the main part of the house where the other family members spend time. This can be a rug, a folded blanket, one of the many styles of dog beds found in dog supply stores, or his crate. During meals or when friends visit, the command to Corky is "go to your place." A chew toy or a biscuit treat should always be there while he's learning. Every time he walks away from it, take him back to his "place." Give him a chew toy to work on. When he can be released from his place, return to him, praise him, and tell him, "O.K., good dog."

Is Your Dog House-Trained?

Does your dog have accidents in the house? Is that the reason Corky isn't allowed to be inside with his family?

The reasons for this problem might be that he doesn't understand

Establish his special place. Put your dog's place where he can see or be with family members.

the house rules, or he can't hold it long enough if he's left alone all day, or he was housetrained where he used to live but can't relate it to his new home. Some dogs as puppies were left in crates too long at a time and had to go in the crate. Like wolves, dogs don't like to dirty their den place but if it's necessary, it becomes a habit and they go wherever they are whenever the urge hits. What can you do to change this situation?

1. Put your dog on a routine. Corky goes out immediately: when you get up, after his breakfast, before you leave home, as soon as you get home, after playing in the house, after drinking water, and before bedtime. Go out with him. Guide him to the same area each time and wait. Give him praise and a treat as soon as he does his job. If he doesn't do anything in 5 to 10 minutes, take him back into the house. In 10 minutes, go outside again. Keep doing this until you can give him a treat for success. Every time you get to his area in the backyard use the same phrase, such as "do your job," or "be a good dog." It doesn't matter what you say as long as it's the same thing each time. Corky will learn what it means when he associates it with the praise and the treat.

2. Corky must always be supervised in the house. He should be with you or confined in a crate or exercise pen. If neces-sary, keep him close to you on a leash. Do this until you know he understands he must always relieve himself out-doors. This could take several weeks, depending on how long he's had this bad habit.

3. If Corky has an accident in the house and you see him in the act, clap your hands and say "no." Take him outdoors im-mediately and praise him when he's in the yard even if he finished in the house. If you don't see him in the act, do not spank or scold him be-cause he won't connect it to what he did and won't know why you're angry with him. (Don't ever spank your dog for any reason. It lowers his confidence in you because he doesn't understand spanking and doesn't know when it might happen again.)

TEACHING YOUR DOG MANNERS HAS MANY REWARDS

This really isn't as much work as it might appear to be. You do what needs to be done whenever it needs to be done. When your dog can be with you in the family, sharing what is going on, you will learn what a unique character your dog is. You will understand the real definition of "domesticated animal." No other species has the relationship with humans that the dog has. You need to spend time together to discover what this is all about.

The dog who understands his place in the family will respect the leader, know what's expected of him, and be happy and contented.

> **The dog who understands his place in the family will respect the leader, know what's expected of him, and be happy and contented.**

CORKY HAS BASIC NEEDS

All dogs have some basic needs. They include the following:

A Place To Call His Own. This should be close or in a family area. A crate is ideal for this because he can go into it whenever he wants to rest or escape from rambunctious children. He can also have a pad or blanket in an area close to the kitchen or in the living room, as in the photo on page 41.

Food And Water. The food should be readily digestible with all the necessary nutrients. If his coat isn't shiny or in good condition try another brand. Always read the ingredients on the bag and compare them. The cheapest isn't always the best. If the dog's condition doesn't improve, see a veterinarian. WATER should be available 24/7. A dog's body has basic needs and they increase with activity and hot temperatures. He should have a water bowl both inside and outside the house.

Is this mine? Every dog should have his own food and water bowl.

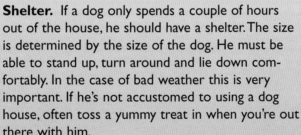

A doghouse provides shade and protection from bad weather.

Shelter. If a dog only spends a couple of hours out of the house, he should have a shelter. The size is determined by the size of the dog. He must be able to stand up, turn around and lie down comfortably. In the case of bad weather this is very important. If he's not accustomed to using a dog house, often toss a yummy treat in when you're out there with him.

Grooming. Dogs with short coats need brushing at least once a week. This removes dead hair and puts a lot of it in the garbage instead of on the furniture. Some with longer hair get matted clumps. These should be combed out while they are very small. Large mats are painful for the dog because they pull on the skin. It's a good idea to take the dog to a groomer if you can't take care of the mats yourself. Toenails are also an important part of grooming. Long toenails make walking uncomfortable.

All dogs need regular brushing and nail trims.

chapter six

CORKY AND YOU HAVE MUCH TO SAY

People and dogs communicate in many ways.

Imagine you are Corky. As a dog, you would probably understand many human words, and you would use your body to communicate. Feel what it's like to run with four legs, to show joy by bouncing in tight circles, to invite a play session with front legs on the ground and rear-end up in the air. Feel hot cement and soft cool grass on your paws.

Get down on Corky's eye level. Look at the world from his perspective: a robin hopping on the ground, shoes and legs coming toward you. Sniff the scents that keep your nose to the ground—cookie crumbs dropped by Jimmy, footprints from Tux the cat, and a mouse who had been there first. To you as a person they might not be so great, but to you as Corky, they're wonderful.

While you are in his mind, how do you express yourself with no hands and no language? How do you show happiness? How do you demonstrate to your person that you're not stubborn, you just don't understand what you're supposed to do? How do you stop someone from hurting you? What if they don't understand?

As a dog, you may understand as many as 100 human words, maybe more, and you certainly understand "down," "come," "no," and "bad

A play bow is a dog's invitation to play.

dog." (When you were a puppy, you even thought that was your name.) You will automatically use body language to communicate with your people because it's the natural thing for a dog to do. But humans don't pay attention. They don't know what you're saying.

Now become Corky's person again and consider what he might be telling you—without being able to speak in words you understand.

DOG LANGUAGE IS WOLF LANGUAGE

Certain signals when used by wolves are called "cutoff" signals because research biologists saw that they cut off aggression in other wolves. When used by wolves, these signals are strong, obvious and consistent—a necessary part of survival because they help wolves to communicate within the pack and avoid fights. This is especially important during the hunt and when sharing the meat after the hunt. Wolves injured in fights can't help with future hunting, and the rest of the pack can't kill enough deer or elk to keep them strong.

We call these signals "calming signals." Wolves use them. Dogs have inherited them. You can take your dog to Thailand, Germany, Peru or any other country. You might not understand the language the people speak, but Corky can communicate with dogs wherever he goes. Dog signals are universal.

CORKY HAS MUCH TO SAY

Since the world of the dog is so different from the wilderness world of the wolf, dog signals vary in degree or intensity and have broader meanings. Watch carefully so you can understand dog language. Sometimes a dog's signal is so quick you miss it. Many of the signals involve slight movements of the head, eyes, lips, tongue and eyebrows. Even though you play with dogs, you might not have noticed these signals because you didn't know about them.

There are over 400 dog breeds recognized throughout the world. These breeds have many different physical characteristics. Not all dogs can do all of the signals. Flop ears, cropped ears, short muzzles, hair growing over the eyes, no tail or very short tails may prevent dogs from making some of the signals. Some dogs are out of practice because they have not socialized with other dogs.

Signals are activated by interactions with other dogs and people. Some medium and large size breeds use signals more commonly than the smaller breeds. There can be a difference between individuals within a breed. But, the more you watch, the more you can catch a glimpse into the wild heritage of your canine friend. You won't take dogs for granted any longer.

> **Signals are activated by interactions with other dogs and people.**

CALMING SIGNALS

Turid Rugas, in her studies of dogs in Norway, has identified thirty different signals. She states that the term "calming signal" is more appropriate for dogs than the wolf's "cutoff signal" because they are used by dogs to prevent threats from other dogs and people. The signals are used to calm fears (the dog says, "I won't fight you") and to make friends. Dogs also use the signals to calm themselves when they feel stressed.

Identifying Calming Signals

Here are some of the more common signals. Sometimes these signals are dog-to-dog, and other times they are dog-to-people. You will soon be able to tell the difference. Knowing and understanding these signals will help you to understand the dogs that you meet and to work together with your own dog.

HEAD TURNING is an obvious and commonly used signal. Some dogs will turn their heads when a rambunctious dog approaches to slow him down. If you're in a park and a dog sees you approaching, you might see his head turn. Another place to watch for this is at an off-leash play area for dogs. Moving the eyes from side to side is similar in meaning to head turning.

Sometimes, a dog will turn his head if he feels uncomfortable or vulnerable. Your dog might turn his head away from you at times. If you lean over him and pat him on the shoulder and he turns his head away from you, he is probably telling you he feels uncomfortable. Although you don't know it, you are unintentionally signaling your dominance, and he is signaling that he's not a threat to you. Leaning over the shoulder area is a sign of dominance from dog to dog or from a person to a dog. If you change your body position and don't bend over him any more than necessary, he won't feel the need to calm either you or himself.

A Springer Spaniel in an obedience class turned her head away from her person every time he leaned over to praise or pet her. Then she would be hesitant to do the next activity. By turning her head, she was telling her person that she felt frightened by his display of dominance. The instructor suggested that he stop leaning over the dog and instead reach out his arm to pat her on the neck and shoulder. Her response to this change was to become a happy partner with him in the class.

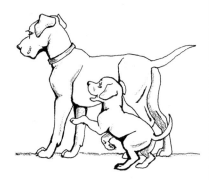

TURNING THE BODY SIDEWAYS TO ANOTHER DOG is a stronger signal. A dog will do this when another dog, often a younger one, gets too rowdy in play. He is saying to the puppy, "Stop jumping on me," or "Slow down."

SNIFFING INTENSELY at the same spot on the ground is another strong calming signal a dog might use. This is a different type of sniffing than checking for the smells of other dogs or dropped food. If someone approaches walking fast to get past him, Corky might put his nose to the ground to calm the person walking by or to calm himself. Sniffing is also used to calm another dog that is fearful or is approaching too quickly.

LIP LICKING is a relatively common but not often noticed form of greeting. With many dogs, it's merely a flicking of the lips. Sometimes the tongue is barely visible, a thin pink line between the lips. This is often a sign of affection, used when greeting the dog's person when they return home. Other dogs' tongues curl toward their noses so far that you can't miss it. You might see this signal when you greet and pet a dog that doesn't know you, or when someone new greets your own dog. He wants to signal that he won't growl or bite, or, if he is a sensitive dog, he will use it to calm his own nervousness. A slower licking relaxes the dog when a stranger approaches and a quick tongue is a happy greeting to a good friend or his person. Many dogs lick just once or twice at a time. Watch closely for lip licking. Sometimes it's hard to see.

Molly, a Shih Tzu (a breed from China) who was a therapy dog, visited Bill in his wheelchair. It had been a long time since he'd held a dog and he felt a little awkward. After Molly was lifted into his lap she looked up at Bill and began lip licking. When Bill began to pet her, she settled into his lap, no longer using her calming signal because Bill had relaxed.

YAWNING is a commonly seen signal. Many people think it means a dog is bored, but it also has other meanings. It can be an expression of insecurity when a dog can't figure out what you're doing or what you expect from him. Between dogs, it can be used to show friendliness, such as a dominant dog to a submissive one.

When you see a dog yawning in any situation, think about what it might mean. Over a period of time, these observations will help you understand a dog's body language. It's a good feeling to connect with what a dog is saying.

You might see a yawn when you're teaching Corky to walk on a leash or to "stay." If you expect him to learn more quickly than he is able to, your impatience and loud tone of voice cause him to feel confused. When you relax, use a pleasant voice, and once again show Corky what to do, he becomes more confident of what you want from him and the need for a yawn disappears.

These body language signals can have any one of several meanings, so how do you know which one a dog is communicating? Think about what is going on at the time and about what the dog is doing. The more you observe dog signals, the better you will understand them and the better you will understand Corky and other dogs. It's a good feeling to connect with what a dog is saying.

Is this mother dog, Snowflower, yawning because she's bored? Probably not. It could be for any number of reasons. The puppies are settling down but they could have been very active, jumping and crawling over each other and their mother. She decided that's enough and tells them to calm down. Or, if you and a friend are laughing and talking, she could be telling you to calm down and not make so much noise. She might be calming herself. "I've had enough of these pups. I think I'll leave for awhile." If you were there when the photo was taken, you might know of some other reasons for her to be yawning. Perhaps the photographer was too close or moving too quickly.

When you see a different dog yawning in another situation, think about what it might mean. Over a period of time, these observations will help you understand a dog's body language.

Watch for Other Calming Signals

You might see other calming signals when you use the "come" command. If you call Corky and he not only comes slowly but in a wide curve, you might get annoyed because you think he's doing this just to irritate you. Actually, he's using two other calming signals. These signals, a *curved line* and *slow approach*, are Corky's way of calming you. Think about how you are calling him. Do you get excited when he doesn't come immediately? Do you jump up and down and shout his name again and again as he slows to a walk? Corky is trying to tell you that he understands but would like you to calm down.

WARNING SIGNALS

Dogs will usually give warning signals when they are feeling threatened, uncomfortable, or even aggressive. Understanding these warning signs will go a long way to prevent you from being injured or frightened by your own or someone else's dog.

In a group of people gathered together after a musical program at school, a boy slept in a wheelchair. His father, busily talking to a friend, held the leash of a dog that was probably a companion or helper to the boy. Several people standing close by were totally involved in talking. No one paid attention to two little girls, probably about ages three and five, who spied the dog and dashed over to it.

The dog *lowered his ears* (1) the first signal that he was uncomfortable. The girls tried to pet him, laughing and getting down beside him. The dog *turned his head* (2), lowering his shoulders, the second sign that he was feeling stressed. He was trying to avoid the girls. They wanted to hug him, one on each side. He *crouched down* (3), trying to *crawl* (4) under the wheelchair. He was on a leash, so he couldn't get away. The two giggling girls tried to get their arms around him even though he was partly under the wheelchair. The dog was cornered and couldn't escape. He had given the girls four signals to leave him alone which, of course, they didn't understand. Fortunately, their mother came and got them, probably

WARNING

Understanding these warning signs will go a long way to prevent you from being injured or frightened by your own or someone else's dog.

When you see a dog standing like this, you know he's ready to fight. See those ears and tail straight up? The other dog doesn't want to fight, Notice the submissive dog's ears and tail.

not a moment too soon. The situation that dog was in could have resulted in a snap, if not a more serious bite.

The lips, ears and tail can be used as warning signals to stay away. These are easy to recognize. Have you seen a dog *curl his lip* (5)? It's usually the front and a corner of his lip, but sometimes his front teeth show. This is used by Corky as a warning to another dog or person to stay away—Corky won't share his chew toy. If a dog *growls* (6) at a member of his people pack it's a sign that he thinks he's the leader of the pack, or he wants to be. This dog needs obedience training so he can learn that you are top dog. If a dog's *tail is up and stiff with the tip quickly flicking* (7), he is feeling aggressive. This is another sign that

Corky is ready to fight another dog, if necessary, or perhaps defend himself from someone who is swinging a stick at him. If a dog's ears are leaning back (8) he's worried; if they are back against his head (9) he's fearful. If cornered, this dog could be a fear biter. If his ears are stiff and forward he's feeling aggressive and may be ready for a fight.

Reading a dog's body language is a fun thing to do. Whether you know the dog or he is a stranger, being able to understand what he's telling you is a good feeling. Put yourself back in Corky's place. How happy Corky will feel now that he knows his person can understand him! All of us should try to watch dogs closely enough to learn what they are telling us with their body.

YOU CAN USE THESE SIGNALS TOO

Know for sure that your own or strange dogs read every bit of your body language. You can use some of these signals that dogs use with each other to communicate with your own or other dogs. When you see either an excited or shy dog walking towards you, turn your head and begin walking toward him in a curved line. As you get closer, ask if you can pet him, approaching him from the side. If you're playing with a dog or puppy that gets too rambunctious, turn your back, fold your arms and don't look at him for a minute. This should calm him. Dogs are very social animals and if they can't get your attention they will stop trying.

CAN YOU IDENTIFY THESE WARNING SIGNS OF AGGRESSION?

1. Which dog is snarling? _____

2. Which dog is showing signs of aggression? _____ Why?_____

3. Which dog may be a fear biter? _____

4. Which dogs are in a serious dog fight? _____

5. Which dogs are play fighting? _____

The answers are on page 94.

Turning away from your dog will calm him down.

In the family pack, you can use dog language effectively with a socialized dog that is well integrated into the family. Learning about dog language can bring you and your dog closer together.

If you're trying to read and Corky keeps pestering you, try yawning. If you see no effect after eight or ten yawns, it's not working. Try again another time. Other dogs will begin to calm down after only a few yawns.

YOU COMMUNICATE THROUGH BODY LANGUAGE

Just as Corky communicates with you through his body language, you communicate with him, even though you might not realize it. He also gets your messages through your thoughts, your hands, and your voice

Dogs notice your slightest movements. Did Corky see you look at the leash or the door or your coat? He will respond to any one of these even if you hardly moved your head. These are signals that tell him you're taking him for a walk and he'll pester you until you clip on the leash and open the door.

Which of these dogs is safe to approach? Which ones are not, and why?

1. A dog that has his ears back.

2. A dog that is sleeping or eating.

3. A dog that appears calm, friendly, and is giving good eye contact.

4. A dog that appears fearful.

5. A toy breed dog.

The answers are found on page 94.

HOW TO APPROACH A STRANGE DOG

You will use dog language every time you meet a new dog. Always observe a dog's body language before you touch him. If the dog curls his lip or stiffens, or moves his ears back, he's saying you're too close and he doesn't want to be touched. Do not approach a dog when he is eating, or startle him by touching him when he is sleeping. Always ask permission to pet someone else's dog. Listen to any comments from the dog's person. If you receive permission to pet the dog, always approach from a side angle, not face on, which might be considered a challenge. Extend your hand with open palm and let the dog sniff you before you attempt to touch him. Some dogs do not like to be patted on the head. Instead, touch them under the chin or on the neck and shoulders.

If the dog turns his head away, he's telling you he's uncomfortable. Perhaps your hand is too high and he doesn't want you to pat him on his head. Perhaps you're standing too close and leaning over him. The dog reads this as dominating. Talk softly, tell him he's a good dog, scratch behind an ear, stroke him on his neck or along the side of this body. Feel him relax. If the dog is bouncy let him lick one hand and stroke him with your other hand.

Approach a strange dog from an angle with your arm extended, palm up.

When you get home from school, your body language tells him if you're tired or have a sore muscle from gym class. Your eyes tell him if you're sad or angry. He will know if you're ready to play by how fast you go to the kitchen for something to eat, and how fast you talk.

YOU COMMUNICATE THROUGH CONCENTRATION

Another form of communication from you to your dog results from concentrating. This means that you think only of what you want Corky to do at that moment; for example, you'd like him to stay

close to you. Corky senses this. He shows his happiness by wiggling and bouncing, watching and coming close. You love the feeling that for a few minutes you two are the only two in the world.

When you focus on what you are doing, you picture it in your mind. Many people who train dogs believe that dogs think in pictures. When both the person and their dog concentrate this way, it's a form of communication.

YOU COMMUNICATE THROUGH TOUCH

Dogs need to be touched. They like it. They have become dependent on humans for their social needs, and touch is one of the most important of these. If they aren't touched, petted, and stroked often enough, they act out in various ways. They might bark too much, urinate in the house, chew magazines or other items, or always demand attention, jumping up or poking your arm.

When you have your hands on your dog, you give him the message that you care, that he's one of

the family and that you love him because he's your dog. Dogs have individual needs for touch. Some are independent and are ready to leave after a short time. Others will totally relax, eyes half closed, and might fall asleep.

If your dog shies away from any touching, even gentle strokes, it might be that he was played with too roughly when he was young. Stressed dogs avoid eye contact, lower their heads, flatten ears, or roll on their backs. You can teach any of these dogs about gentle touch by giving yummy treats in one hand and stroking with the other. Begin with just one minute of stroking, or even less. Begin on the neck and over the shoulders. Stroke the length of the body. Your dog will let you know what feels good.

Your dog will also enjoy some gentle massage. Use two or three fingers and rotate the finger tips in very small circles. Corky can be either lying down or sitting. Move the massage circles from his shoulders to his hip, just below his spine. You can also use your fingertips on his front shoulders and upper rear leg. Corky might want to leave after a short time, or he might take a snooze. Let him tell you what's best for him. Always remember to do this gently.

YOU COMMUNICATE BY TALKING

Probably you talk a lot when your dog is with you, in the same room, out in the yard or on a walk. But how often do you talk directly to Corky, giving him specific information? He doesn't understand all the words you use but he gets the message. One clue he gets is from the tone of your voice. Another clue is from the picture in your mind when you are talking to him. Remember to use a happy voice, not an angry or pleading one.

A good kind of talking to your dog is to tell him when you're leaving the house, where you're going and when you'll return, such as a simple "Wait. I'm going to school and I'll be back this afternoon." You might think this is silly, but with repetition it calms Corky. "Wait" is a command that means "stay here around the house." When you use the same words each time, he learns that you always come home.

Ask him if he wants to go for a walk, if he needs to go outdoors, if he's ready to go to bed, if he wants to play ball. He will learn all these different words and will continually become more bonded to you. Add more words by naming each toy and each trick and each part of your daily routine. "Do you want to take out the garbage?" Soon, the word "garbage" will mean something fun to him. He'll perk up his ears or maybe his eyebrows, wag his tail, and if he could he'd say, "Sure, let's go."

chapter seven

WHY DOES CORKY DO THAT

> **Dogs are social animals who need to be with people. Problem behaviors often come from confusion.**

What is the most miserable thing that can happen to a dog? To live isolated from his family, his pack, tied in the yard or living full-time in a fenced pen. The agony comes with being alone. The only contact is when a member of the pack brings food and leaves again.

What Corky wants is to do his job, being his people's companion. When a dog can't do this he gets into trouble. When he gets into the house, he often runs and jumps and plays too rough. Worst of all, he isn't housebroken. This is how dogs end up in animal shelters.

Take a walk through an animal shelter. When you first arrive, the barking dogs sound far away. Then you open the door. A rolling surf of barking floods the air. Wire kennels with sides six feet high line both sides of the room, with another row down the center. Each space houses one or two dogs.

A brown dog with long silky hair, his tail wagging slowly, walks to the door of his wire cage. The big dog in the pen next to his bounces off his wire door, long tongue hanging half way to the floor from barking so loud for so long. The little brown dog stops wagging his tail, goes to the back corner and curls up with his nose under his tail.

Keep walking. The barking frazzles your brain until you can't think. But you can see each dog's eyes

watching you. Soft brown eyes begging for affection. Puppy eyes—happy, wanting to play. Angry eyes that warn, "Stay away." "Take me home" eyes belonging to a dog that is rubbing his shoulder against the wire gate to get your attention. Sad, "I've been here too long," eyes. Too many of those eyes. You can't look any more.

Why are these dogs here? What did they do that was so bad?

Some were left because the family moved and couldn't take their dog with them, while others were brought here because their person could no longer care for them for some very good reason. But many are here because they weren't taught how to behave and live with people.

THE DOG'S JOB HAS CHANGED

Differences Between Breeds

The wolf carries all the working abilities that we see in the genetic makeup of dogs. This is what makes him such a remarkable animal. Breeders through the centuries have taken an individual quality of the wolf and selected for that in their dog breed. Sight hounds are superior in seeing birds and animals from a distance. Scent hounds are superior at tracking animals for long distances. Herding dogs instinctively keep a herd of animals together, taking them where the farmer directs. Other dog breeds were bred selectively to do different jobs: finding pheasants and other birds, catching rats, pulling wagons filled with produce to market, or guarding the home or livestock. Every breed of dog originally had a purpose, a job to do.

Originally dogs were bred to do specific jobs. Retrievers were developed to retrieve birds for hunters.

For most dogs that has changed in the twenty-first century. The job of most dogs today is to be a companion to their people.

Whatever a dog was bred for originally is still in his instincts, still a part of his natural abilities. Most dogs adjust easily to being a companion because the dog is the most domesticated of all the animals, including the cat, and has bonded to humans for longer than memory. Dogs accept people, recognize their different moods, and seem to know when they're needed for a hug or a long walk. Interacting with family members is the most important job a dog can have.

The people in the family pack can help the dog adjust to his new job. It is our responsibility, as leaders of the dog's family pack, to learn about our dog's natural instincts and talents. When we understand better what makes dogs tick, we can relate to them in ways that keep both people and dogs happy. The instincts discussed in Chapter 4, which were bred into various breeds, are what cause dogs to behave as they do. Knowing why and how problem behaviors are triggered can help us help dogs to control these behaviors. Some examples of problem behaviors follow.

SCENTING

With their noses, dogs identify friends, strangers, good guys and bad guys. Their scenting ability opens them to a world we know nothing about. When they are scenting in the outdoors they are in the world of the wild. We can teach them what we want them to find, but once they begin, whether ground scenting or air scenting, they function on their own. In that world they are superior to their human pack members. Their scenting (olfactory) ability makes them valuable in identifying drugs, explosives, and people in collapsed buildings or buried in avalanches and in searching for lost children and hikers.

WHY IS MY DOG BEHAVING THIS WAY?

PROBLEM BEHAVIOR: **Circling** children or other dogs at play and sometimes nipping at their heels; **Chasing** joggers.

Instinct that drives it: Herding.

What sets it off? A group of active children or small animals like chickens or puppies.

Type of dog: Collies, Corgis, Border Collies, Australian Shepherds, Australian Cattle Dogs, Shetland Sheepdogs, and mixed breeds who have one of these breeds in their bloodlines.

PROBLEM BEHAVIOR: **Growling** or **Snapping** when you reach for his toy or food dish or when you try to move him off a chair or bed.

Instinct that drives it: Pack order. Challenge for family pack leader.

What sets it off? Living in a family in which no one is the leader so the dog takes the job.

Type of dog: Can be an individual dog in any breed. Rottweiler, Chow Chow, and German Shepherd, originally bred for guarding and protection, are prone to this behavior, but other breeds may do it, too.

PROBLEM BEHAVIOR: **Chasing** small animals, squirrels and rodents. **Digging**, looking for mice and moles underground.

Instinct that drives it: Prey

What sets it off? A running squirrel, the scent of a mouse.

Type of dog: Any of the Terrier breeds or mixed breeds with Terrier as part of their combination, or dogs of any other breed.

Terriers love to chase squirrels and other small animals.

PROBLEM BEHAVIOR: **Mouthing** (pulling on sleeves or arms with the mouth to get attention, but not clamping down with the teeth)

Instinct that drives it: Pack behavior, to get attention on his terms

What sets it off? In puppies, these actions are normal. In an adult dog, this can be a major nuisance when he wants your attention.

Type of dog: Can occur in any breed. Even very small dogs can become problem mouthers unless they are taught not to mouth at a young age. If they are older, they can still be taught, but it takes longer.

Dogs should be taught not to grab a person's arm, leg, or clothing while playing.

Puppies use their mouths to learn about the world. They must learn not to mouth or nip when they are very young.

Do not permit this type of behavior. Distract the puppy with a toy.

PROBLEM BEHAVIOR: **Nipping** (snapping, using teeth but not breaking the skin)

Instinct that drives it: Identifying the world with the mouth.

What sets it off? Puppies use their mouths when they are learning about their world. Some nip as well, when they are startled or if they are beginning to protect their food dish. If puppies are not trained early, they continue this bad habit as adults.

Type of dog: Any dog can exhibit this behavior.

PROBLEM BEHAVIOR: **Biting**. This means breaking the skin, a very serious problem.

Instinct that drives it: Guarding.

What sets it off? Whether the cause is with the aggressive temperament or personality of the dog, or the biting is a result of how the dog has been treated, teased or abused, the family should seek the help of a dog trainer or animal behaviorist. **Ask your veterinarian for a recommendation.**

Type of dog: Dogs bred for guarding; dogs of other breeds with a dominant or aggressive personality.

PROBLEM BEHAVIOR:

Pulling on the leash

Instinct that drives it: Combination of hunting (what's out there?) and pack behavior (who's in charge?).

What sets it off? High energy, tempting sights and smells—Whoops! There goes your arm down the street, still attached to your dog, still trying to pull him back and slow him down. Is your dog going to wait for you to catch up and put yourself back together? No. The dog must learn good behavior from the pack leader and other members of the people pack.

Type of dog: Can be any breed or mix of breeds. Even a tiny Terrier can drag you after him when he gets up a head of steam.

Dogs should never be allowed to pull on the leash.

PROBLEM BEHAVIOR:

Failure of Housebreaking

Instinct gone awry: Pack behavior. Though dogs and wolves naturally want to keep their personal area clean, dogs need to be trained for a larger indoor area like a house.

What sets it off? Not understanding the difference between indoors and outdoors. This can happen if your dog wasn't totally trained as a puppy. You have a job ahead of you, an important job. Dogs need to be with us in the house whenever possible. If your dog urinates and poops on the carpet, the adult leader will be very unhappy and will keep the dog in a confined space or outdoors. You can re-train the dog, but you must be very consistent. It will be well worth the effort. (Refer to Chapter 4 for guidelines.)

PROBLEM BEHAVIOR:

Nuisance Barking.

Instinct gone awry: Nuisance barking is different from barking when someone comes to the door, when the dog wants your attention, or when your dog is simply greeting you. Instinctively used to warn of danger or change, barking by lonely, isolated dogs is a cry for companionship. This barking is the saddest of all. Once they begin to bark, they keep on.

What sets it off? Some breeds (hounds, guard dogs, Terriers) are bred to bark. But dogs, like their wolf ancestors, are social animals. They live in a pack. Spending every day alone stresses many dogs and they begin to bark. Training your dog to control barking is discussed in the next chapter.

Type of dog: Dogs of any breed.

PROBLEM BEHAVIOR:

Not Coming When Called.

Instinct gone awry: Pack order. Dogs who have a leader know their place in the group, but some dogs fail to acknowledge the family leader.

What sets it off? Smells of the sidewalk, the grass, or other dogs who have been in the same area. The dog doesn't recognize the person who is calling him as having a higher pack order, so the person is ignored. Dogs need to be trained to COME when they hear that word. Practice this command in different areas, including places with distractions.

Type of dog: Dogs of any breed.

These are the problems most often seen in the neighborhood dogs and in our own canine companions. All of these problems can be corrected with some effort on your part. In the next chapter you will learn about some tools that will help let your dog know which behaviors you like and which ones you want him to change.

chapter eight

TEACH CORKY GOOD MANNERS

Don't grumble about training your dog. It's a good way to get to know him better. The reverse is true, too. Your dog will learn more about you, which is good. You both will learn about tolerance and patience. This can be a plus for living in a family pack.

You don't need big chunks of time for training. That's drudgery. Dogs love to play—to be happy. Take advantage of that. Show Corky that he can play, stop, pay attention, practice what you want him to do, be happy doing that, and then get more play time. Each dog is different, so you'll need to figure out how best to do this with Corky.

Did you notice that several of the problems in the last chapter resulted from dogs not understanding their place in the family pack? They don't know who's in charge. This causes a

While you're training, rewarding Corky with a treat and praise is necessary, but a pat on the shoulder or the chest tells him he's part of the pack.

REMEMBER:

NO chocolate treats. Chocolate is poisonous to dogs.

dog to be uncertain about what is expected from him, which can make him hyperactive, irritable (growling or not wanting to be touched), or always getting into mischief. Every dog has his own list of mischievous activities.

HELP CORKY UNDERSTAND THAT YOU'RE IN CHARGE

By the time you have taught Corky the commands, "sit," "down," "stay," "come," and how to walk on leash, you have learned which of his buttons NOT to push that create problems. You're a team and each knows who's in charge and when. Yes, there are times when your dog knows best: when a stranger is at the door, when another dog is safe to approach, when a storm is coming (before you know it), and when you don't feel good and need a friend. Because commands are needed by Corky in the human world and because you're a member of that world, you're the teacher.

The Nose – A Number-One Training Tool

It's worth a lot to find a treat that your dog loves. The secret to speedy learning is his nose, not his stomach. Smell is his strongest sense. It's how he learns all about his world and identifies most of it. Try small pieces of hot dog, bacon, cheese, chicken, or dog food that comes in a roll and can be cut into pieces. See if he has favorites. Use these when you begin teaching him. Later, when he knows the command fairly well, you can treat randomly with treats like Cheerios or popcorn.

Another plus to yummy-smelling treats is that Corky's brain associates that pleasant smell with you. He feels good when he works with you, even when you treat randomly. Once he begins to learn a command, *give a treat only when he does the command correctly.* If he does it incorrectly, tell him to "try again." He will quickly learn what that means.

Some dogs respond better to a toy as their reward. Small and soft is best so it can fit in your pocket until it's time for the reward.

It's important for you to stay calm when training. If you become cross and give your dog a harsh correction, he will become fearful because he hasn't learned yet what the command means and doesn't know what he did wrong. When you keep your cool and simply correct him, he will learn.

TEACHING THE "WATCH ME" COMMAND

To begin with, make Corky feel happy when he pays attention. Do this in the house whenever he's close to you. Say his name in a happy voice. The instant he looks at you, praise him with gusto.

Here are some pointers to help you teach the "watch me" command:

- Corky sits or stands close to you, on leash, either beside or in front.

Teaching the "watch me" command. When your dog responds quickly to your hand signal, use only the words "watch me."

- Have a treat in your fingers and move your fingers to your eye. If you can't get his attention, make smoochy-type noises. Say, "Corky, watch me." The instant he looks up at you, give him the treat and praise him.
- When he understands what you want, keep him looking at you a few seconds longer. Make faces, wiggle your head, whatever works to keep him looking at you. Praise while he's still watching you, so that you're the one who

gives him permission to stop watching you.
- *Always* stand. If you get down on his level, in his mind you're no longer the leader; you're only his playmate. If your dog is small, put him on a table while he is learning this command. This puts him close to your face. Keep him on the table for just a minute or two, watching him carefully so he doesn't run around. Keep his leash on. You can also teach him to focus on a place on your leg at his eye level. Mark it with a piece of colored tape. Use your fingers to teach the location of the spot. Rub the spot with a piece of cheese or hot dog to catch his attention.
- **YOU** must pay attention. If you call his name and begin thinking of something else, or talk with a friend, Corky gets no feedback from you. If this happens a few times, you've shown him it doesn't matter if he pays attention to you or not.

When a dog has learned "watch me," use the command to get eye contact any time you need to communicate with him or keep his attention on you rather than some distraction in the environment.

RULES OF THE HOUSE

The commands that are most helpful in teaching Corky to live comfortably in the family pack are "sit," "down," "stay," and "come." When he knows these commands, you will both be happier. You have learned how to teach Corky to "sit"

and taught him to go to his special place in the house. Now Corky is ready for some additional lessons.

Control Barking

Dogs bark to warn of someone approaching or of danger, and sometimes for other reasons, but you want Corky to be quiet when you tell him to. This is important so that Corky does not disturb other people or become a nuisance to your neighbors.

- When Corky barks, tell him "quiet" or "enough." Distract him with a hand movement. Give a treat when he stops barking.
- Teach him to bark on command. Tell him "bark," then quiet him after he's barked three or four times.
- After Corky has learned this command pretty well, stop giving him a treat every time. Do give him random treats.

The "Down" Command

This command means "lie down" and is a continuation of the self-control learned with "sit." Some dogs don't want to go down, but it's important for all dogs to learn this. (If your dog jumps up on people, say "off" so he won't get confused with the "down" command.)

- Guiding with a treat gives Corky a positive attitude. Move the treat from his nose to between his front feet. Put your other hand on his shoulders as you slide the treat out in front.
- With some dogs, put the treat between their legs so that their heads tuck to get to it. When Corky is down, quietly praise him and pet him for a few seconds.

The Down Command. Your dog's nose should follow the treat to the ground. If his tail end pops up, push it down.

The "stay" command or "down stay." Put your foot on the leash while you move out in front. If he tries to get up, it will pull and stop him. This helps teach him that "stay" means "don't walk away."

Put your foot on the leash as soon as you return. Corky must learn not to jump up until you say, "Good dog."

The "Stay" Command

For this command, you will need to have Corky on a leash. The method is the same as for the "sit" and the "down." When Corky will sit or lie down at your side quietly for a minute or two, you can begin the "stay." He has to be able to stay because he wants to be there. You can stroke him and talk to him to keep him by your side.

- Put the palm of your hand in front of his muzzle. Tell him to "stay" and swing around in front, facing him. The first "stays" should be only about 10 seconds.

- Swing back to him, count to three, and release him with "O.K., good dog."
- Gradually extend the length of the "stay" to 30 seconds and then to a minute. If Corky tries to move, quietly put him back where he was.

The "Sit Stay" Command. Use a hand signal to remind your dog to stay. Once or twice is enough. If he stands up, use the leash to put him back in the same place.

When you return, praise him without letting him run and jump around.

- After you have successfully increased the time, start gradually moving back until you reach the end of the leash. Now you can lay the leash down and walk further back. If he moves, quickly walk to him and put him back exactly where he was. Never call him to you when you're teaching the "stay."
- Always return. "Stay" means "stay here until I return."

It's important to stay calm when training. Harsh corrections or an angry tone of voice can make a dog fearful.

The "Wait" Command

The "wait" command is more relaxed. Use "wait" when you leave Corky in the house or the car (except in the summer, when it's too hot for dogs to be in closed cars) or at the door when you don't want him to go out ahead of you. This keeps you in control.

- When you're at the door, about to go out, have Corky on leash. Tell him to "sit" beside you at the door. Then tell him to "wait." If he gets up and tries to go out, have a helper shut the door quickly, or use the leash to have him sit beside you again. Close the door and repeat, "wait." When he obeys, praise. Do not give him a treat.
- When you're coming inside and want Corky to stay out, tell him to "wait" until you get through the door.

When you leave your house give your dog the kind of chew toy you can put treats in. Each time, use the same sentence to tell him you're leaving and will be back.

The "Come" Command

This command must always be obeyed. It could save Corky's life someday. You want better than a 90 percent response when you call Corky. You want him to come as soon as you call him. One of the ways you can get this kind of response is to always have a favorite treat in your pocket. After you've called Corky a few hundred times (not on the same day) using a treat, then you can begin to use a treat occasionally. This command is very useful if your dog gets distracted when you are walking him.

You can use either a retractable-lead or a leash to teach this command. The techniques are different.

Using the retractable-lead:

- When Corky is ahead of you, call "Corky, come" in a firm, pleasant voice. Put your thumb on the button that stops the line. When he turns and looks at you, say "good dog" and take your thumb off the button. The line will roll in as he comes to you.
- On the first try, Corky might run on past, headed for something exciting on beyond. Bring him back to you. Do a "sit" and "watch me." Praise him with your voice. No treat. Tell him, "O.K." and begin walking. When he's away from you, repeat. Call him again. If he comes straight to you, praise and give a treat.
- If he jumps on you, looking for the treat, ask him to do a "sit" and "watch me." Corky should know the "sit" command very well by now. Praise. No treat. Repeat.
- At the next "come," give him a "sit" command just before he reaches you. Corky soon learns that you hold a treat in front of you at his eye level or tucked into your belt. When he gets close, tell him to "sit," give the treat, and praise.
- For a short dog, mark the front of your leg or pants with white or black tape or a clip. Rub with the treat so Corky can smell it. Point to it. If he jumps up when he comes to you, looking for the treat, do a "sit" and "watch me." Praise. No treat. Repeat. Give a treat this time if he sits correctly.

Using the six-foot leash:

- Put your dog on a "sit-stay" or have a friend put three fingers under the collar. Walk to the end of the leash and face your dog. Call, "Corky, come."
- Run back a few steps to encourage him, and stop when he's close. Tell him to "sit." Praise and give a treat. Repeat if necessary, with lots of praise and a treat when he gets to you.
- You can also teach the "come" when you're walking your dog. Even if he's busy sniffing, call "Corky, come" and give a quick tug and release on the leash. After he comes to you, continue walking.

On the six-foot leash, when your dog gets distracted on the "come," run backwards a few steps to get his attention.

Your hands give Corky a focus.

When he gets close to you, give him a "sit" command. Praise and treat.

Using the "come" without a leash:

- When Corky is coming every time you call him, try calling him with no leash. Begin in a fenced yard or in the house and stay close, no farther than 8 or 10 feet from him at first. Because he's off-leash, you must have success or he'll quickly figure out: no leash; no come.
- If he ignores your command, clap your hands, call his name, jog a few steps to get his attention.
- If he looks at you, praise him for looking. If he still doesn't come, lie down on the ground or hide behind something. Most dogs will go to you to find out what happened to you. Now you know you need to do some more training with the leash. Are you using one of Corky's favorite treats every time you call him? That's very important. Maybe not to you—but when you live with a dog, learn to think like a dog.

WALKING ON LEASH

When you are in a natural area, a field or forest, and your dog surges ahead, he is excited by his hunting instinct. He searches for exciting smells and sometimes seems to be overwhelmed by so many. If you're walking in your neighborhood or on a city sidewalk, Corky sees new and interesting things and new smells to investigate. You could end up flying behind him, bumping and crashing into other people. Not fun.

When your dog isn't paying attention and is pulling on the leash, turn and walk in another direction. Don't change your pace. Your dog will feel a tug on the leash and turn towards you, hurrying to catch up. Praise him when he gets to your side. If you do this consistently and often, he will soon learn to return to your side whenever he feels a tug on his leash.

Remember the four things you can do to keep Corky from forging ahead and dragging you. Mix them up each time you walk him.

1. Call "come" when he reaches the end of the leash.
2. Turn in a different direction.
3. Change your walking speed—slower, faster, zigzag.
4. Stop walking. Wait until he returns to you, then continue walking.

The pull on the leash lets him know you've changed direction. Don't say anything. You want him to learn to pay attention to what you're doing.

Walking on Leash. When your dog begins to pull, turn and go another direction.

He will soon catch up. If you get in the habit of walking him on your left side, he will always know which side to go to.

Running games are good exercise for your dog.

Run in curves so that Corky will pay attention and try to keep up with you.

If he bumps you, stop immediately. That ends play time. He will soon learn not to knock you down.

"CATCH ME"

"Catch me" is a fun way to get Corky's attention. It means action. Corky runs to catch up as you zig and zag. Then you laugh, praise him, and pat him on his shoulders and sides. This is important, because touching by his pack members helps Corky maintain a well-balanced attitude to other people and dogs in his life. While you're training, rewarding him with a treat and verbal praise is necessary, but a pat on the shoulder or chest tells him he's part of the pack.

"Catch me" satisfies his need to be part of a group and gives you a quick game to play as a reward for good behavior while you're teaching commands.

GUIDELINES FOR TRAINING YOUR DOG

1. Be patient. On one day, Corky does so well that you know he knows the "sit" or "down" command. The next day you're annoyed because he acts like he's never done either one before. Dogs have ups and downs while they are learning a command. This is a normal part of the learning process. Just like you when you can't remember something new you learned a week ago, Corky sometimes forgets a new command. It usually takes about five weeks for a dog to master a command.

2. Losing your temper or shouting angrily, or constantly jerking the leash, will only confuse Corky, and make it even harder for him to remember what to do.

3. When you praise, use the name of the command you are praising: "Good sit! Good down!"

4. Praise Corky whenever he does something you like. This does not need to be a command. He can be lying on the floor beside you when you do homework.

5. Have fun. Play with your dog.

6. Use treats. Put some treats in your pocket. Using treats when you train speeds up the learning process. Dogs are motivated by a treat. They know you're the leader and they love having fun with you, but when it comes to working or learning something new, they learn more quickly when there's a food incentive.

7. If you're using a toy as a treat, remember that Corky must let go of the toy when you say "enough" or "stop." Do not allow him to play tug of war with it.

8. When Corky begins to anticipate a command, begin giving treats or toys randomly, perhaps every second or third time he obeys. Eventually, your voice, praise and pats will be enough for Corky.

Once Corky is comfortable with these rules, he will be a better behaved companion.

TRAINING EQUIPMENT

Collar: A buckle or snap collar. Not tight, but shouldn't pull off over the head. Should always have an ID tag and a rabies or license tag.

Chain collar: Use only when training or walking your dog. If Corky pulls so hard that he sounds like he's strangling, don't use this collar. It can damage the larynx in his throat. Review the training steps for walking on a leash. If Corky wears this collar all the time, it can get caught on something, get twisted and choke him.

Head Collar: Very good for large dogs or dogs of any size who always pull. Some dogs don't like to have it put on over their nose. Practice with Corky. Give him bits of his favorite treats while you take it on and off his muzzle. Have a helper give treats while you put it on. Corky should be wearing a neck collar with leash attached, and your foot on it, to keep him from moving away from you. If he can't get comfortable with wearing the head collar, then do not use it.

Harness: Good for smaller dogs. Doesn't give the control of a neck collar, but some dogs prefer the harness and are calmer on walks. A regular harness works well for this. The front-clip control harness is a favorite for leash walking. It is sold with different brand names, SENSE-Ation Harness, Sensible Harness, K9 Freedom Harness, and Easy-Walk Harness. The main difference with this harness is that the leash attaches in front of the dog instead of over the shoulder.

Leash: Nylon leashes work well if they aren't too thick and stiff. The same is true of leather leashes. They will soften up and be comfortable and flexible to use. Of course, puppies and young dogs like to chew them in half. Retractable leads allow Corky to move farther away from you, up to 16 or 26 feet. This gives him more freedom. It takes practice to control Corky and bring him back to you when you are around other people and dogs. It's great to have one of these when you're walking in a more open area, but it shouldn't be the only leash you have. A regular 6-foot leash is best for sidewalk walking.

---

chapter nine

YOU, YOUR DOG, AND FUN, FUN, FUN

You can do fun games that imitate in some way a part of the behavior that an instinct creates.

Some dogs seem to have a higher energy level than others. This can be part of the normal behavior for their breed, which also depends upon their size and the job they were bred for. Terriers, for example, are quick on their feet and always alert for anything they might want to pounce on and grab when out for walks. They are full of energy and love to be around their people.

Dogs are continually being stimulated by their instincts. Whatever the basic energy level of any dog, it will be increased whenever the dog is stimulated by an instinct. This includes seeing people and animals who "need" herding, small animals who "need" to be chased, a mailman approaching the house who "needs" to be barked at, or a stream or puddle that "needs" to be jumped into.

When Corky isn't allowed to use his instinct, he still retains the physical energy that the instinct aroused. He doesn't know what to do with all that energy. Some families have a phrase for this: "There goes Corky, flying around the ceiling." He runs around the house; he bounces off his family pack members. He wants to go on a walk when everyone else is watching TV. When he does go for a walk, he bolts out the front door. The unlucky person at the end of the leash flies into space behind him. Add this

energy to a high-energy personality and you've got a super-powered dog.

FUN GAMES TO PLAY

How can you help Corky release the extra energy that comes from suppressing his instincts? You can do fun games which imitate in some way a part of the behavior that an instinct creates. Whether your dog is a high-energy type or not, these games are fun. Enjoy playing with your dog, and be careful not to overdo. He'll let you know when he's had enough by not paying attention. Learning tricks can be mentally tiring to a dog.

1. **At home, you can play the *find* it game.**
   - Use the "stay" or have a friend hold the leash, or tie it to a chair leg.
   - Hide a biscuit or a toy. Let Corky watch you the first few times.
   - Walk back to him, release him and tell him to "find it." Until he reaches the point where he doesn't need to watch you hide it, help him if necessary.
   - Stand close to the place and point. If he begins to lose interest, clap your hands to get him excited.
   - Praise him vigorously when he finds the object.

Be sure that your dog's balls and toys are large enough that he will not choke on them.

2. ***Bounce a ball.***
   - Get in front of Corky.
   - Bounce a ball, one that fits in his mouth, so that it comes down close to him. He learns to catch it in mid air. If you bounce it too hard it will go too high and be difficult for him to keep track of and catch.
   - When you begin, stay just a few feet away and bounce it so it will not go far over his head. This game is best played outdoors, in a fenced area.

3. **Play *hide and seek.***
   Even though this is a fun game, don't expect Corky to know how to play without some practice first.
   - Have someone else hold his leash or distract him while you go out of the room or behind a piece of furniture when he isn't looking.
   - Call him: "Corky, come." Repeat, "come."
   - Make some noise. If you're behind a piece of furniture, pat the floor (but not so hard that the lamp wobbles back and forth).

- If someone else is in the room, he can direct Corky toward you. As soon as Corky stumbles into you, give a treat and lots of praise.

You can gradually go farther away when you hide. You and Corky will love this game. But if you go too far, such as into one room and through a door into another room, before he understands the game, it won't be fun for Corky any more and he'll stop looking for you.

4. Let Corky *retrieve*.

Some dogs are born chasing a ball; others have to learn what fun it is. Here are some tips to help him enjoy it.

- Get Corky excited by waving a ball or a soft toy in front of his nose. Toss it a few feet. Every time he sniffs or touches with his nose, praise and treat.
- Play this way each day until he picks up the ball. Make a big happy fuss when he does this.
- If he begins to grab the ball and run off with it, tie a 20-30 foot cord to his collar.
- Hold the line loosely, close to the dog. *Don't wrap it around your hand.* You might get pulled down on the ground.
- Drop the line on the ground as soon as your dog takes off. Run after it. When he reaches the ball or toy, pick up the line or stand on it. The purpose of the line is to keep Corky from running farther away. Talk to him.
- Try running in the opposite direction to see if he will follow you. Whenever the line gets a little bit loose, gather it in until you've folded the looseness in your hand. Don't pull him in like a fish, because he won't learn anything that way.
- When Corky finally gets to you, take a treat from your pocket. If

he drops the ball on his way back to you because he's in a hurry for a treat, don't scold him. You're teaching him to return to you. After he learns that, you won't give him a treat unless he brings the ball with him.

5. Teach the *box* game.

- As your dog sits and watches, put a treat in one of two boxes (or bowls) that are different in size, not too large, and different shapes if possible.
- Repeat the treat in the same box several times while Corky is watching you. Then put the treat in the second box several times. You might want to do one box one day and the second box the next day because with too much repetition he might get tired of it.
    - Then on another day put the treat in one box at a time, with your dog watching each time. Corky will learn that the treat can be in either box.
- The next step is to let Corky watch while you put it in one box and move the boxes around in circles, back and forth, so they're not in the same place next to each other.
- Tell him to "search." Let him find the treat. When he understands this, put a cloth over the top of the box after the treat goes in and move the boxes to different positions. He will use his nose to choose which box has the treat and will get under the towel, newspaper, or whatever you use as a cover.

TRICKS

Tricks are fun. Dogs like them because the people are happy and the dogs get treats and/or praise. There are many tricks you can teach your dog, like rolling over, playing dead, sitting up on his haunches, walking on his hind legs, barking on command, learning to count (bark the number of times you ask), dancing, catching a frisbee, and more. Following are just a few of the tricks you can teach Corky.

1. Biscuit on the nose

Most dogs with long enough muzzles seem to like the biscuit-on-the- nose trick. Have your dog sit. Tell him to "wait," which is a good command to use for this. Put the biscuit on his nose, repeating "wait." In a few seconds tell him "O.K.," or "get it." Dogs have different ways of tossing the treat and catching it.

2. Shake

Here's a quick way to teach "shake hands." Put a treat between your thumb and your fingers and put it down next to his foot. When his paw touches your hand, immediately give the treat. If he hesitates, touch his paw first with your hand. Begin to say "shake" or "high five" each time. Advance to giving a treat only when he raises his paw when you ask him to "shake." When he raises his paw every time, give a treat every few times and finally, praise only. He will act like he's done something wonderful, and he has.

> **Tricks and games are fun for Corky and may help develop his intelligence.**

3. The crawl

Put your dog on "down." Be on your knees beside him, with a treat on the floor just in front of his nose. Slowly move the treat on the floor a couple of inches. He will stretch to reach it. Move it just a little bit farther the next time until he has to crawl to get it. If his rear end pops up, push it down with the palm of your hand. Be patient until he learns what you want him to do.

Don't put the treat too far away. In this photo, Peaches isn't interested because she can't see the treat.

Once she sees the treat, Peaches follows it.

4. *Winding between the legs*

Teach your dog to circle your leg by guiding him with a yummy treat. If he quits, put the treat at his nose. You have changed hands. Now you can go around your other leg if you want to.

You might think these games and tricks don't have anything to do with a dog's instincts. But finding a hidden dog biscuit or toy or person uses scenting and hunting. Playing with a ball relates to retrieving game (meat) and bringing it to the den. Waiting at the front door, staying in his place and other commands you've taught him relate to the pack instinct and paying attention to the pack leader. These games and commands can help your dog overcome his high energy and learn to live more calmly with you.

chapter ten

THE HISTORY AND FUTURE OF THE DOG

They have so much to teach us and we have so much to learn.

From the time humans and dogs came together, there has been a special sort of bonding between them. This increased when the dog, using his instincts and natural abilities, worked with humans in hunting, farm work, herding, pulling carts and protecting the home. Sometimes it was a dangerous adventure that created the bond. The story of John Muir and the remarkable dog, Stickeen, is a striking example.

John Muir was one of the great early naturalists. He was a principle person in making Yosemite into a National Park and in organizing the Sierra Club. A lover of dogs, he believed that they had many of the same emotions as humans but also had strong connections to the wild. He believed that a dog was a unique individual who could teach humans something about themselves and about the value of experiencing nature.

He was in Glacier Bay, Alaska, in 1879, and went back to explore some of the glaciers in 1880. He stayed at Fort Rangell, where he met Stickeen, a little brown dog who didn't want attention from humans, didn't come when called or sit with people around the campfire, but who attached himself to Muir on his explorations.

On this first hike they covered seven miles of ice in a snowstorm. Stickeen flew easily over crevasses that gave Muir pause. On their return hike they came to a fifty-foot-wide, 1,000-foot deep crevasse that could be crossed only by way of a knife-edged bridge eight to ten feet below the glacier's surface. Finding another way around was not a choice in the worsening storm. With his ice axe Muir cut narrow steps down the vertical wall and then a six-by-eight-inch platform from which he could straddle the needle of ice that stretched across the chasm. Smoothing the edge in front of him, he moved across in a buffeting wind. When he reached the other side he carved a set of narrow steps and finger holds to the top. He wrote in his journal later that he had never before been under such a deadly strain.

On the other side, Stickeen began to cry in distress. After trying several ways to coax him, Muir called from the edge of the crevasse and told Stickeen that he had to leave but would return in the morning to save him. He told the dog to stay away from the woods because the wolves would kill him. After this lecture, Stickeen gathered up his courage and inched his way down to the platform. Cautiously he stepped on the narrow ice bridge and braced himself against the wind, only to stop in fear when he reached the narrow deck on the far side. He hesitated, measured the steps, and then sprang up the wall and launched himself into a manic celebration. Never before or since had Muir seen anything like Stickeen's release from despair into uncontrollable joy.

From that time on Stickeen was a changed dog. He stayed close to Muir, ate only when Muir fed him, laid his head on Muir's leg in the evening and looked into his eyes as if to say, "Wasn't that an awful time we had together on the glacier?" The shared experience of danger had bonded and altered him, Muir wrote, "making Stickeen less wild, more whole, more complete, more domestic and giving him a deeper sympathy for his fellow beings."

POEM ON A HEADSTONE AT NEWSTEAD ABBY, ENGLAND

Near this spot
Are deposited the
Remains of one
Who possessed Beauty
without Vanity,
Strength without
Insolence,
Courage without
Ferocity,
And all the Virtues of
Man without his Vices.

This Praise, which would
be unmeaning Flattery
If inscribed over human
Ashes,
Is but a just tribute to
the Memory of
BOATSWAIN, a DOG
Who was born in
Newfoundland May 1803
And died at Newstead,
Nov. 18th, 1808.

George Gordon, Lord Byron.

Through the years and in many villages and towns, dogs have been honored for their faithfulness and perseverance. In the 1930s in Japan, an Akita, Hachi-ko, always greeted his owner (a professor at Tokyo University) at 3:00 p.m. every afternoon at the Shibuyu subway. One day, however, the dog waited in vain because the professor had suffered a fatal stroke. The determined Akita returned day after day to await the return of his master. Visitors came from all over the country to pet the famous dog. A bronze statue was erected to honor his faithfulness and long vigil. After nine years of waiting the dog finally collapsed and died of old age at the base of the statue.

These stories tell of the bond between humans and dogs, a connection that has existed for many centuries. Dogs have touched the lives of humans in all kinds of ways.

So here we are, full circle. We began with the domestication of the dog from the wolf and conclude with the dogs we live with today. It's been a long path for the dog. Some of the time the dog had to find his own food and shelter because his human did not have enough to share. Some humans were cruel and kicked and beat with a stick if the dog couldn't work hard enough. But as the hundreds and thousands of years went by, the dog, with his sharp senses, learned to read humans—their gestures, their movement, and their tone of voice—so well that he could adapt to living with humans. Even subtle movements that we might miss, the dog can pick up. This ability has made it possible

As you play with and train your dog, a special bond develops.

for dogs to adapt to living with humans and to stay with them.

In recent years, most dogs have come to live a very different life than they did even fifty or sixty years ago. People loved their dogs back then, but they were not part of the family the way they are now. Interest in the dog as a subject of research began earlier, but only in the areas of anatomy and physiology. Research on the behavior of dogs and why they do what they do was not of enough interest nor was money available to proceed.

One of the first studies of dog behavior in this country took place in Jackson Laboratory, Bar Harbor, Maine, by John Paul Scott in the 1940s and 50s. It revealed different behaviors among each of five different breeds of dogs. Beginning in 1946, Scott, along with

CHANGES IN THE DOG

The major changes in the dog while becoming domesticated were internal. These were identified in the Russian Fox Experiment and can also be applied to the dog. Their effects took place in the hormonal system and brain chemistry, causing permanent changes in the behavior of the dog. The wolf has a fear of humans or anything that was suddenly different in his environment, such as a large tree that had toppled across a familiar pathway. These types of fear changed in the dog with the lowering of the level of the adrenal hormones. At the same time, seratonin hormone levels became higher in the dog's brain and this lowered the intensity of the levels of aggression. Perhaps this is related to bite inhibition in dogs. These changes and others identified in the Russian Fox Study are some of the reasons that dogs and humans eventually developed a companionable relationship.

his research associates, discovered the canine critical-development periods and proved, through controlled research, that puppies must be mentally stimulated early in life (from birth to 3 months) to achieve their full potential. Scott's studies created a revolution in the dog world. People didn't believe that young puppies were able to learn. After Scott, along with Clarence Pfaffenberger, developed puppy classes and temperament tests for Guide Dogs for the Blind, testing became an accepted practice. We can thank them for sharing their knowledge for all the families who can help their dogs to be the best they can be.

Today, most dogs cannot run freely the way Rocky and his pals did in their mountain town. Instead, the dog's person takes him outdoors on a walk. Today, the dog is not ignored 24/7, except for being fed, but is part of the family after they are home from school and work. Dogs are often taken to training classes and taught how to live with the family, how to obey commands, and how to do many activities. Training, as we have seen, makes a big difference in how happy both the dog and the family are together. Some kinds of training can teach the dog to aid us and to do ever more complicated tasks. The best part is that the dog is working, as he was bred to do, which helps to calm his excess energy. He isn't overly excitable as he is when he has no purpose or job.

Another thing that has changed is how dogs and people relate to each other. Dogs share our lives in so many ways; we know now that we need to let our dog be a dog and share our lives in his own doggy way, letting him sniff on walks, taking him where he can run, and playing games with him. We know that we need to enjoy dogs as they are. Dogs have so much to offer us and to teach us.

What makes the dog so special? For one, his keen instincts and genetic heritage give him the ability to come up with new ways to help his human companions, like warning of an epileptic episode. For another, his senses, especially scenting, are so refined that he can sniff out explosives and concealed drugs of all kinds. And as we have seen, dogs are sensitive to their humans' behavior and emotions.

We know that dogs have emotions such as sadness, anger, joy, loneliness, excitement, and fear. Once you

THINGS TO REMEMBER:

open your eyes to see what your dog is telling you, once you know his language and can understand him better, your relationship with your dog becomes a unique bond that we share with no other creature.

From ancient to modern times, dogs have been our helpers and companions, and we have now begun to discover just how amazing the connection between humans and dogs can be. It is a unique and precious bond—*and that's why the dog is so special.*

- Touch your dog every day.
- Groom him regularly.
- When you leave him alone, provide toys, chewies, or toys stuffed with food to keep him busy.
- Make sure your dog gets adequate daily exercise.
- Observe dogs. Learn to communicate and read their body language.
- Encourage him to use his senses and his inherited abilities.
- Take time to socialize, train.

And most of all—PLAY AND ENJOY EACH OTHER

Afterword

From this book you've learned that dogs, while they have a wild ancestry, want more than anything to be our companions. You've learned some ways of helping them be happier in the world of humans that they have chosen to live in. You've learned how to understand better what they are saying to you, and how to communicate with them. And best of all, you know now why the dog truly is "man's best friend."

What a wonderful time you and your canine companion (or a dog you know or might have someday) can have together, now that you understand each other so well. You can go for walks, play games, do your chores around the house, and just hang out. All that time, you'll be doing your job of being his trusted leader and he'll be doing the job of being your companion.

A TRIBUTE TO THE WOLF AND TO THE DOMESTICATED WOLF — YOUR DOG

The way to understand your dog is to understand the wolf a little better. You can do this by reading books, watching nature programs on TV, and visiting a wolf preserve whenever possible.

Vast differences are obvious. The wolf is wild and his main focus is on survival. Instincts in the wolf are very powerful. The dog is domesticated and his main focus is on his people. Instincts in the dog vary in strength but they are present in all dogs. They're the source of differences in personality traits of the various breeds. Many of the differences between breeds have been brought about by the selection process similar to the Russian experiment discussed in Chapter 2. But no matter what the breed is, there's still some wolf in the dog.

If you ever have an opportunity to attend a program given by members of a wolf preserve, do your best to go. At a program held at Colorado State University in Fort Collins, Colorado, members of the audience got a thrill when the director of the program from Mission Wolf told the audience that if the wolf felt comfortable enough with the people, she would lead us in a group howl. We should begin very softly, and the wolf might join in. This would end the program.

A gentle sound of a hundred voices floated softly into the air as the audience began to howl. Within a minute, the wolf felt comfortable enough to raise her head with an equally gentle tone. She led the chorus. The song grew in a variety of tones. The rhythm changed, the volume grew, the room filled with one of the first voices in the history of the animal world leading a chorus of voices from the present. Music filled the room, each person shivering with the joy of the blended voices.

By degrees, the tones softened as the group followed the lead of the wild singer. When silence returned, the man and the wolf left the room. We sat quietly for a few moments absorbing the beauty of what had just happened. Perhaps we were so moved because of our connection to the dog, descendant of the wolf.

And as we, the people who have become the dog's main focus in life, come to enjoy and appreciate the nature of the wolf, we will also be a better friend and partner to this faithful creature who has given so much to us.

GLOSSARY

Adaptation. The adjustment of living creatures to environmental conditions in terms of food and climate.

Agility. A sport for dogs that involves one dog at a time running a course of a variety of equipment designed to demonstrate physical ability and working cooperatively with the handler.

Ancestry. The line of descent that shows a dog's relatives by name or breed and can be traced back thousands of years, such as to Egypt.

Avalanche. An area of snow that slides down a mountain side, increasing in speed and depth, and taking everything in its path.

Breed. A group of dogs related by descent from common ancestors and who are visually similar in most physical characteristics and natural abilities.

Cytoplasm. The substances inside the cell wall and surrounding the cell nucleus.

Distemper. A highly contagious viral disease in dogs which can be prevented by a vaccine.

DNA. The molecular basics of heredity that are located in the nucleus of the cell. This is the DNA used to identify individuals by law enforcement agencies as well as victims from a catastrophe such as an earthquake.

Mitochondria (mtDNA). Structures that exist within the cytoplasm of the cell. These structures have their own DNA which differs from the DNA in the nucleus of the cell. That DNA comes from both parents. mtDNA is passed down only from the mother dog to her pups. (This is the same in humans, also.) The purpose of mitochondria is to convert fat, protein and carbohydrates to energy which is delivered to all cells to use to sustain all activities of life.

Gene Pool. The gene pool has to do with the traits of a breed. A prehistoric gene pool refers to the genetic content of dogs in a particular location in the world that breed with each other.

There is enough similarity within the large group to identify them as a gene pool. In current times some breeds are small in number. A small gene pool has less diversity within the gene pool which can cause an increase in health problems within a breed. Good breeders are very careful to select healthy dogs in their breeding program.

Genetic studies. A branch of biology that researches heredity and the genetic makeup of humans and animals.

Hieroglyphics. A system of writing in picture script used by ancient Egyptian priests before writing as we know it.

Ice age. An historical era 10,000 to 12,000 years ago when the Northern Hemisphere was covered with ice.

Immigrant. A person who goes to another country to take up residence. It can also be an animal who moves to a new environment.

Industrial Revolution. A period at the end of the 18th century when power driven machinery was introduced along with a major change in the economy of a country, such as England.

Leash laws. A community ordinance or law that requires a dog to be on a leash when it is not confined to its family's property.

Neuron. Brain cells with specialized procedures that send energy messages to other cells in the body for their physical and mental functions. These are delivered through the nervous system by pathways and branches coming from each neuron.

Pack. A group of predatory dogs with strong prey instincts who run together, or it can be a group in a breed, such as a pack of hounds, who are trained to run together for the purpose of hunting. Wolves live in family packs, often of six or eight members, but can be larger.

Predator. An animal that hunts and kills other animals for food.

Prey. An animal that can be attacked by a predator for food.

Socialization. A term that describes the process of training a dog to adapt to its social needs in relation to people and other dogs.

Wolf. The European Grey Wolf, from the ice age and earlier, is the ancestor of the dog. The American Timber Wolf, with which we are familiar, is not an ancestor of the dog. Modern field studies using GPS and telemetry show different pack behaviors in the Timber Wolf than did earlier studies.

ANSWERS TO QUESTIONS

Chapter 4, Page 36:
Identify Ways to Socialize Your Dog
A. Sit and Stay
B. Tunnel
C. Play
D. Hike (or walk)
E. Fetch
F. Tricks

Chapter 6, Page 51:
Identify Warning Signs of Aggression
1. Photo D (Curled lip and exposed teeth warn "Stay Away!")
2. Photo E (Tail up and stiff, barking, lowered ears.)
3. Photo A (Tucked tail, ears back, fearful stance.)
4. Photo C
5. Photo B

Chapter 6, Page 52:
Which Dogs Are Safe to Approach?
Number 3. A dog that appears calm, friendly and is giving eye contact is generally safe to approach. Greet him calmly from an angle, with your palm extended.

A dog that has his ears back is saying he does not want you to come closer.

Dogs that are sleeping or eating do not like to be disturbed and might bite if startled.

A fearful dog might snap or bite rather than turn and run.

Toy breeds are sometimes snappy. Their small size makes them feel the need to protect themselves.

Abrantes, Roger. *Dog Language.* Naperville, Illinois: Wakan Tanka Publishers, 1997.

_____. *The Evolution of Canine Social Behavior.* Naperville, Illinois: Wakan Tanka Publishers, 1997.

Askani, Tanja. *Kinship in the Wolf: The Amazing Story of the Woman Who Lives with Wolves.* Translated from German. Rochester, Vt.: Park Street Press, 2006.

Bergin, Bonnie. *Understanding "Dog Mind."* New York: Little, Brown, 1995.

Brackman, Jane. "The Canine Conundrum." *AKC Gazette,* December, 2004. 42-45.

Bradshaw, John. *Dog Sense: How the New Science of Dog Behavior Can Make You A Better Friend to Your Pet.* New York: Basic Books, 2011.

Clothier, Suzanne. *Bones Would Rain from the Sky.* New York: Warner Books, 2002.

Coppinger, Raymond, and Lorna Coppinger. *Dogs.* New York: Scribner, circa 2001.

Coren, Stanley. *How Dogs Think.* New York: Simon and Schuster, 2004.

_____. *How to Speak Dog.* New York: Simon and Schuster, 2000.

_____. *The Intelligence of Dogs.* New York: Macmillan, 1994.

_____. *The Paw Prints of History.* New York: Simon and Schuster, 2002.

Csanyi, Vilmos. Trans. Richard Quandt. *If Dogs Could Talk.* New York: North Point Press, 2005.

Darwin, Charles. *The Variation of Animals and Plants Under Domestication. Vol.1.* New York: D. Appleton and Co., 1883.

Derr, Mark. *Dog's Best Friend.* Chicago: University of Chicago Press, 1997.

Fogle, Bruce. *The Dog's Mind.* London: Pelham Books, 1990.

Grandin, Temple, and Catherine Johnson. *Animals in Translation.* New York: Scribner, 2005.

Green, Susie. *Talk to Your Dog.* New York: Sterling Publishing Co., 1995.

Katz, Jon. *The New Work of Dogs.* New York: Random House Villard Imprint, 2003.

Kerasote, Ted. *Merle's Door.* New York: Harcourt, Inc., 2007.

Lange, Karen E. "Wolf to Woof." *National Geographic* January 2002. Vol. 201 Issue 1, 2.

Lindsay, Steven R. *Handbook of Applied Dog Behavior and Training, Volumes 1 and 3.* Ames, Iowa: Iowa State University Press, 2000.

Link, Mike, and Kate Crowley. *Following the Pack: The World of Wolf Research.* Stillwater, Minnesota: Voyageur Press, 1994.

McConnell, Patricia B., Ph.D. *The Other End of the Leash.* New York: Ballantine Books, 2002.

McMillan, Franklin. D., DVM, with Kathryn Lance. *Unlocking the Animal Mind.* Emmaus, Pennsylvania: Rodale Press, 2004.

Miller, Pat. *The Power of Positive Dog Training.* New York: Wiley Publishing, 2001.

Mills, Cynthia. "Dogs of Rarotona." *Discover Magazine*, June 2004 Vol. 25, No. 9, 70-77.

Ostrander, Elaine, Urs Giger and Kerstin Lindblah-Toh. *The Dog and Its Genome.* Cold Spring Harbor Laboratory: 2005.

Page, Jake. *Dogs: A Natural History.* New York: Harper Collins.

Rugas, Turgid. *On Talking Terms with Dogs: Calming Signals.* 2nd edition. Kula, Hawaii: Dogwise Publishing, 2006.

Savaleinen, Peter. "mtDNA Studies of the Origin of the Dog." In The Dog and Its Genome.

Serpell, James, ed. *The Domestic Dog: Its Evolution, Behaviour and Interactions with People.* Cambridge, England: Cambridge University Press, 1995.

Thayer, Helen. *Three Among the Wolves: A Couple and Their Dog Live a Year with Wolves in the Wild.* Seattle, Wash.: Sasquatch Books, 2004.

Trut, L.N. "Early canid domestication: The farm-fox experiment." *American Scientist Research*, Triangle Park: March/Apr. 1999. Vol. 87, Issue 2, 160-169.

Voith, Victoria, DVM, Ph.D., and Peter L. Borchett, Ph.D. *Readings in Companion Animal Behavior.* Trenton, New Jersey: Veterinary Learning Systems, 1996.

Askani, Tanja. *Kinship in the Wolf: The Amazing Story of the Woman Who Lives with Wolves.* Translated from German. Rochester, Vt.: Park Street Press, 2006.

Birmelin, Immanuel. *How Dogs Think: A Guide to a Beautiful Relationship.* New York: Barnes & Noble, 2007.

Clutton-Brock, Juliet. *Dog.* London, New York: Dorling Kindersley. Eyewitness Books, 1991.

Coren, Stanley. *The Intelligence of Dogs.* New York: The Free Press, A Division of Macmillan, Inc, 1994.

Grogan, John. *Marley & Me.* New York: William Morrow, An Imprint of HarperCollins Publishers. 2005.

Halfpenny, James C. *Yellowstone Wolves in the Wild.* Helena, Montana: Riverbend Publishing. 2003. www.riverbendpublishing.com

Leonard, Jennifer and Carlos Vila. "From Wolf to Domestic Dog." Article in *The Dog and Its Genome*, ed. Ostrander and others. Cold Spring Harbor, New York: Cold Spring Harbor Laboratory Press, 2006.

Lingenfelder, Mike, and David Frei. *The Angel by My Side.* Carlsbad, California: Hay House, Inc. 2002.

O'Neill, Amanda. *Dogs.* New York: Kingfisher. 1999.

Rugas, Turid. *On Talking Terms with Dogs: Calming Signals.* Second Edition. Wenatchee, Washington: Dogwise Publishing, 2006. www.dogwisepublishing.com.

Savaleinen, Peter. "mtDNA Studies of the Origin of Dogs." Article in *The Dog and Its Genome,* Cold Spring Harbor, New York: Cold Harbor Laboratory Press, 2005.

Thayer, Helen. *Three Among the Wolves: A Couple and Their Dog Live a Year with Wolves in the Wild.* Seattle, Wash.: Sasquatch Books, 2004.

ABOUT THE AUTHOR

Clarice Rutherford has co-authored two books, *How to Raise a Puppy You Can Live With,* and *Retriever Puppy Training –The Right Start For Hunting.* She has lived with dogs much of her life and been active in obedience, hunt tests, field trials and tracking.

She says she is continually amazed at the variety of abilities and the wide range of personalities that exist in the dog world. They have been her best teachers. The canine friends she has rescued, rehabilitated and given a foster home have been both purebred dogs and those of mixed ancestry. Some have taken weeks to overcome the physical and mental abuse from their previous humans. A few have stayed and joined her family. Their problems and age were too deep for them to be able to adjust to another new home.

She lives in Colorado with her husband, Bill, and two Labrador Retrievers, Patrick, a yellow, and Brenna, a black.